Topographic Psychology

Behavior and the Geometry of the Brain

Charles Raymond Snow

Trafford
PUBLISHING

For my maternal grandmother, Dominga Navarro Morales.

Table of Contents

Introduction

Why do people behave the way they do? Why does a species that produces sublime works of literature, science, art, and music also produce crime, murder, war, and genocide?

In the industrial west, answers to these questions have been proposed by philosophy, political ideologies, psychology, and religion; but none of these responses has been adequate. That's because they've all been couched in terms of the self, the mind, or the soul; but I propose that the correct framework is the body.

"That doesn't make sense," you may think. "People behave badly because they make poor decisions; decisions are made in the brain, not in the body."

But what if you have to decide whether to stop the machines that are keeping alive a loved one who's been comatose for years? At such times, you feel your heart racing, your cheeks flushing, and your stomach knotting up. That's because thinking and decision-making are firmly rooted in the body; they're biological processes. So, in order to understand why people make bad choices, we have to investigate the biological basis of cognition.

Our most powerful tool for understanding all things biological is evolution. Evolution is the biological consequence of the fact that what happens today is mainly an outgrowth of what happened yesterday. In the light of evolution, biology largely has been transformed from the study of life to the study of the history of life.

If we reconstruct this history by relying exclusively upon the fossil record (and ignoring microscopic species that, during the Archaean and Proterozoic Eons, diverged and subsequently rejoined,) then the history of life can be depicted as a tree that has a single root and many branches, with the root

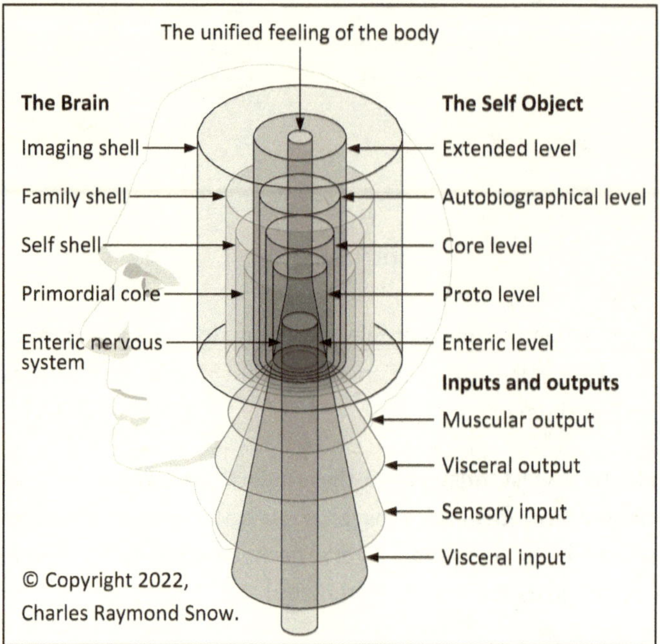

Figure 1: A Conceptual Map of the Brain

A vertebrate's brain can be conceived as a biological machine that uses an internal world model to transform sensation into movement. Inhabiting the brain's central axis is an artifact called the self object that represents the animal, itself. Both the brain and the self object comprise five layers that are nested, one within another, like the hollow wooden figures in a set of Russian Dolls.

representing a particular single-celled species that lived 3.5 billion years ago, [1-2] the branch tips representing all of the species (contemporary and extinct) that descended from this ancestor, and the branch points representing the splitting of one species into many. This depiction makes it clear that we're not just human beings; we're also hominins, primates, mammals, vertebrates, animals, and life-forms.

This encapsulation of one taxonomic group by another makes it possible for us to focus, one group at a time, on behaviors that we've inherited from our ancestors. To this end, it's useful to conceive of a second tree, which is isomorphic to the first, that represents the history of the behavioral repertoires of the corresponding life-forms. This parallel history was shaped by the same forces that shaped the history of life.

When examined from this perspective, behavior reveals itself to be an expression of structures within the body and the conduits that connect them. By using the structures and the plumbing of the body, living beings transform sensation into movement, [3] systematically import raw materials from the environment, construct a self, procreate, and cycle between eating, avoiding being eaten, and reproducing. [4]

All living things perform these five fundamental activities; conversely, anything that performs them is alive. [5]

Topographic psychology possesses a single unifying concept: the transformation of sensation into movement. [6] A transition from sensing to moving is called a decision. Decisions that are made in the brain are facilitated by neural artifacts that are derived from sensory input. There are two fundamental kinds of neural artifacts: objects and connections.

Topographic psychology offers a simple but powerful way of understanding the brain: that the brain largely consists of topographic maps that jointly constitute a world model. [7] So, for example, a lion's brain contains a map of its proprietary territory in the external world of the savannah, as well as a map of the bones and muscles in the internal world of its body. As far as its brain is concerned, both maps depict pieces of the same reality.

In addition to these large-scale representations, the lion's brain possesses detailed maps of extra-brain referents. Such a map is called a sensory image. In general, the brain transforms the image of an external referent into a neural artifact called an object, and the image of an internal referent into a state of awareness called a sensation. So, for example, a lion's brain contains objects that represent all of the animals that are known to it, and experiences sensations that represent the states of all of its internal organs.

What an animal decides on the basis of its neural maps is heavily influenced by the disposition of its body, which, at any given moment, is in one of three states: violence, sex, or work. [8]

Topographic psychology is based upon proposals made by Paul MacLean, Antonio Damasio, and Rodolfo Llinás. In particular, it adopts Antonio Damasio's idea that nerves from internal sensory arrays throughout the body converge in the basement of the brain, where their signals unite into a composite feeling of the global state of the body, and that this feeling is the foundation of the internal sense of self. But it further proposes that the nerves, themselves, are the foundation of a neural artifact, which may be called the self object, [9] that maintains homeostasis, reacts to events that impinge upon the body, and represents the body within its owner's thinking. [10]

Topographic psychology suggests a way by which the brain might construct representations of external referents, store an enormous number of them, and enable the thought of one to trigger the thought of another. It also suggests why a cognitive error, once made, is nearly impossible to detect; why one's self-image can be at odds with reality; and how anger or fear can cause a vertebrate to shift from a normal behavior into a more primitive one.

Unlike derivatives of Sigmund Freud's theory of behavior, topographic psychology provides useful insights into heinous crimes. In particular, it asserts that, by and large, murder is committed by men who are either amok or psychopathic.

This difference notwithstanding, Freudian theory and topographic psychology have much in common; both assert that most cognition is unconscious; sex is a dominant issue of life; there are ideas that are innate and universal; and the brain is partitioned into functional areas that manifest as different personas.

Lastly, topographic psychology merges the study of human behavior with the study of animal behavior; this unification enables topographic psychology to bridge the conceptual gap between psychology and neuroscience.

§

Between 1991 and 1999, I attended nine men's religious retreats. I consequently got to hear firsthand the private concerns of 100 good men, and, through them, of their families and local communities. In the ninth year, with the Bishop's approval, I compiled a list of significant matters that had been discussed during the retreats. In all, there were 82, which I eventually resolved into three categories: issues relating to violence, issues relating to sex, and issues relating to work. Subsequent research revealed that violence, sex, and work are the dominant issues, not only of men, but of all forms of life.

Throughout the time span of the retreats, I was employed as a network analyst. In the course of my work, I noticed that a scale drawing of a dense telecommunications network looks like a map of the territory that it serves. This led me to conceive of the brain, which is largely a network of neurons, as predominantly a model of the world. The biological mission of this model is to transform sensation into movement in a way that promotes survival.

Also during this time, I began to notice more and more ways in which brains and computers are alike. That both are able to perform multiple tasks concurrently was already widely known; but, during the course of my work, I encountered many other similarities. For example:

1. By continually switching the body's context between violence, sex, and work, the brain makes the body act like a finite state machine.

2. Color vision in a vertebrate is similar to color graphics in a computer.

3. Nighttime vision in a vertebrate is similar to grayscale graphics in a computer.

4. The representation in the brain of a visual referent is similar to the representation in a computer of a three-dimensional figure.

5. A story or a chain of inference in the brain is similar to a linked list of records in a database.

6. A neuron that possesses a connection to itself in the brain can perform counting and timing like an integrated circuit in a computer.

7. The neural layers of the vertebrate brain are similar to the communications layers of the Internet.

As I encountered more little-known facts about networks, computers, and brains, I came to realize that they could serve as the core of a new theory of behavior; one that was more scientific than Sigmund Freud's, and that, moreover, was sufficiently rich to predict new knowledge. For instance, it suggested that most serious crimes are committed not by one perpetrator but by two.

Introduction

It's now been more than 20 years since I embarked on this adventure. What has emerged is a new theory of behavior that breaks through the miasma that was inadvertently generated by Freud, and that accommodates much of the neuroscience that's been developed since his time. By virtue of its single unifying concept, the transformation of sensation into movement, and its innovative way of understanding the brain, that the brain is predominantly a world model that mediates the transition from sensing to moving, the new theory possesses an internal consistency that's lacking in other schools of psychology.

ş

I'm indebted to my professors at Adelphi University, Donald Hammer and Nancy Iezzi, who obtained a scholarship for me that enabled me to continue my studies.

I'm grateful for the support of my wife, Mary, my brother, Robert, and my friend, Donald Soule; and for the counsel of L. Michael LeBlanc, who edited my early drafts, and John J. Dagianis, who reviewed the first complete manuscript.

I'm also thankful for the hospitality and generosity of the manager of The San Francisco Kitchen, Bastien DiCaprio.

Lastly, I'm grateful to my students at Central High School in Valley Stream, New York, who, by virtue of their genuine curiosity and ceaseless questions, taught me how to explain complex ideas in an accessible way.

Chapter 1: The Geometric Architecture of the Brain

The first virtual reality machines were built in 1978; today, there may be as many as 200 million of them; but the number of people who regularly engage in virtual reality is much higher than that. Every human, and indeed, every animal that has a brain, inhabits a virtual reality; an internal model of the real external world that resides within its brain; a simulation that, despite its being private and unique to its owner, is sufficiently similar to that of a conspecific to enable them to interact.

An internal world model consists of objects, assumptions about them, and connections and transactions between them. Because an animal's behavior largely is determined by the contents of its world model, understanding objects is a prerequisite for understanding behavior. An object is an internal representation of a referent. If the referent is an animal, the corresponding object is called an avatar. An animal's most important object is the one that it references whenever it's attending to its own body; this artifact is called the self object. Because primates, in order to survive, rely mainly upon their sense of sight, visual objects dominate their thinking.

Over the past thirty years, neuroscience has revealed an astonishing number of details about the workings of the brain. Yet we still can't explain how the brain constructs, stores, and recalls a visual object. Much about the process is understood; but what's understood is frustratingly incomplete. Here's what we know:

1. The brain constructs an object by processing a retinal image of an external scene that contains the corresponding referent.

2. The construction takes place within a collection of neurons that connectively form a multi-layered pyramid.

3. The bottommost layer, which is located within the primary visual cortex, contains a nearly verbatim copy of the retinal image.

4. By ascending the neural pyramid, the image is refined in a stepwise manner that involves many regions of the brain.

5. During this refining, irrelevant details are discarded, and the representation of the referent progressively occupies fewer and fewer neurons. [11]

6. While the image is being processed, data is siphoned off and sent to nuclei that immediately generate appropriate reactions. For example, if the referent poses a mortal danger, the hypothalamus launches a body-wide sequence of actions that prepares the animal for fight or flight, and the amygdala produces a feeling of fear.

7. In order to recall the referent, it's likely that the brain traverses, in reverse, the neural pyramid in which the object was constructed, and thereby produces, in the bottommost layer, an approximate image of the referent; because this layer is cortical, the regenerated image doesn't interfere with the one that's currently on the retina.

8. Whenever a referent is recalled, it's likely that the corresponding object is constructed anew; [12] that is to say, like the original image, the regenerated image ascends the neural pyramid. This would explain why many of the feelings and emotions that were elicited during the original construction are re-experienced.

(A neural pyramid more commonly is referred to as a neural hierarchy; in the context of sensory perception, it's conceived as a sequence of increasingly wide receptive fields. It's likely that neural pyramids are laterally compressed, and consequently, are hard to discern.)

It's not possible to understand human behavior without a credible explanation of visual objectification. So, in the interest of proceeding, a speculative explanation is presented in the following paragraphs and is elaborated in subsequent chapters. This explanation is based upon the observations that were listed above and is, I believe, sufficiently close to the truth to serve as a useful mental model.

Because objectification is a biological process, the best way to explain it is to investigate how it may have evolved. A fortuitous benefit of this approach is that it allows the gradual introduction of neurological facts and terminology that are essential to understanding behavior. But the facts are many and the terminology, obscure. So, instead of burdening you in this first chapter with a ponderous lecture, I'm going to tell you a slightly frivolous, confabulated story of how the human brain came to be and how it came to perform objectification in the manner that's described above. Objectification will be given a more serious treatment in Chapter 9.

From this point forward, the word, "animal," will denote an animal that has a brain.

Also, in the interest of simplicity, numeric quantities generally will be rounded to whole number multiples of some power of ten.

ς

The human brain wasn't created by a master planner; it was cobbled together by a jack-of-all-trades who had to make use of whatever was available. Let's give him a name: Harold; and let's transport ourselves back in time to his first day on the job, which occurred a little over 650 million years ago.

Harold recently has submitted the winning bid on a multi-year contract to create the first human being; an animal that not only looks like us, but also acts like us. The contract requires him to comply with the following rules:

1. An amoeba-like protist called a Trichoplax will serve as an initial prototype; the multi-nucleated tissue that it uses for digestion and cell-to-cell communication will be deemed to be its brain.

2. Harold will build a second prototype by improving on the first, then a third by improving on the second, and so on.

3. If he makes a mistake, he must discard his current prototype and start again with the preceding one.

4. Once he's added a part, he may not delete it; he may, however, shrink it over many generations until it becomes insignificant.

5. From time to time, genetic mutations will happen, and he'll just have to fold them into his design.

6. Harold isn't allowed to disconnect the brain from the body of its owner.

7. He'll evaluate each prototype by allowing it to run around for a few years and observing its behavior.

8. He must complete the entire project within 650 million years.

Harold rolls up his sleeves and begins to produce a succession of prototypes.

A Trichoplax performs digestion via the secretion of digestive enzymes and cell-to-cell communication via the secretion of small proteins. The effectiveness of secretion in a Trichoplax makes Harold realize that if a cell secretes molecules into the interstitial space that surrounds it, it can affect events that occur inside the body; and if it secretes molecules into the external environment, it can affect events that occur outside. So, Harold decides to improve his early prototypes by creating cells that secrete new kinds of molecules.

Eventually, Harold produces a prototype whose body is long. In order to enable the animal to see where it's going, Harold moves its main external sense organs to one end of its body. Then, in the interest of efficiency, he clusters together cells that secrete, into the body, identical molecules and moves the clusters to the front end of his prototype. By so doing, he enables them to more easily communicate with each other and more quickly respond to events in the outside world.

Some cells secrete substances that must be transported to remote locations in the body; so, Harold invents the circulatory system and arranges for such cells to dump their secretions near capillaries, through whose cell membranes they can diffuse into the bloodstream.

ς

Then, one day, Harold converts a particular type of secretory cell into a neuron. In general, a neuron comprises a cell body, a tree of short input projections called dendrites, and a long output projection called an axon. In order to enable neurons to receive signals from other neurons, Harold studs their dendrites with mushroom-shaped protuberances called spines.

The strategy of clustering like secretory cells has proven to be so useful that Harold applies it to neurons, too. If a neural cluster is located in the brain, it's called a nucleus; if in the body, it's called a ganglion; but for our purpose, and in the interest of simplicity, from this point forward, the word, "nucleus," will denote any secretory cluster, regardless of whether it's located in the brain or in the body, or whether it's neural or nonneural.

As his prototypes get bigger and more complex, Harold expands the influence of each neural cluster by greatly increasing the number of neurons that connect to it. Most of this additional matter consists of axons, the majority of which are wrapped in a whitish insulating substance called myelin; because myelin is permeated by blood-bearing capillaries, the additional tissue takes on a pinkish color. (However, whenever a specimen of such tissue is preserved in formaldehyde, it looks white; for this reason, tissue in the body that comprises myelinated axons commonly is called white matter.)

If the axon of a neuron in a nucleus connects to a cell that's located elsewhere in the body, the nucleus can send a signal to the cell; conversely, if a cell in the body connects to a neuron whose axon, in turn, connects to a neuron in a nucleus, the cell can send a signal to the nucleus. This arrangement proves to be so useful that Harold begins to connect more and more nuclear neurons to cells in the body.

In order to forestall a hopeless tangle, Harold separates axons that originate in the brain from those that originate in the body, and, wherever feasible, bundles like-destined axons together. Such a bundle variously is referred to as a nerve, a tract, or a fascicle.

ξ

The day arrives in which Harold's most recent prototype is a vertebrate.

In vertebrates (fishes, amphibians, reptiles, birds, and mammals,) nerves that control bodily movement conjugate in the spinal cord, which connects to the brain via a hole in the base of the skull called the foramen magnum. So, henceforth, whenever Harold wants to add to his prototypes a feature that involves bodily movement, he'll have to route a set of corresponding nerves through this hole. As he adds more and more such features, the nerves form a dense mass within the foramen that becomes increasingly difficult to penetrate. After scratching his head for a while, Harold realizes that he can circumvent this complication simply by sliding new nerves along the outer surface of this neural mass. So, that's what he does.

Whenever the earth undergoes a major change, such as the onset of an ice age, it threatens the survival of Harold's prototypes. This compels him to quickly invent a large number of interrelated adaptations. Those that involve bodily motion necessitate a corresponding set of nerves that must be threaded through the foramen magnum, whose diameter Harold periodically increases in order to accommodate them. As he slides these many new nerves along the outer margin of the neural mass in the foramen, they form a cylindrical shell that tightly surrounds it. Consequently, as the earth repeatedly undergoes major changes, the nerves in the foramen arrange themselves into a sequence of nested concentric cylindrical shells, like the hollow wooden figures in a set of Russian dolls.

As these nerves emerge from the spinal cord and work their way into the brain, the neural layers in the foramen are compelled to balloon outward into the skull while maintaining the order of the cylinders from which they came. Consequently, the sequence of nested cylinders in the foramen produces a corresponding sequence of nested shells in the brain.

As Harold continues to connect nerves to the brain, they increasingly get squeezed together. Nerves that are crammed together can develop cross-connections. If such a link enables a signal to jump from its usual track onto a circuit that's of ancient evolutionary vintage, the brain inadvertently may regress to a primitive state and thereby cause its owner to act inappropriately; such derailments tend to occur when the owner is angry or afraid.

This shortcoming notwithstanding, the nested cylinders in the foramen, and the consequent layering of the brain, bestow a great benefit upon the brain's owner: Because the most essential nuclei are also the most ancient, they're located in the innermost shell. This shell tightly surrounds the brain's central axis, which extends from the center of the foramen magnum to the center of the brain. Accordingly, these nuclei are called the axial nuclei.

Because of their central location, the distance between the axial nuclei and all of the others is minimal, and therefore, so is the time that's required for the former to communicate with the latter. This means that they communicate at the greatest possible speed; and in nature, most of the time, speed improves the chances of survival.

The human brain sends out cranial nerves that innervate various parts of the head, neck, and torso, but that don't pass through the foramen magnum. The vagus nerve, for instance, passes out of the skull through another hole, called the jugular foramen. In the interest of brevity, we'll disregard the cranial nerves.

§

A vital system needs protection from traumatic impacts; so, Harold surrounds the brain with the meninges, a shock-absorbing sleeve that lines the inside of the skull, and which, by extending downward through the vertebrae, envelops the spinal cord.

To further protect the brain from violent impacts, Harold causes cerebrospinal fluid from the central canal of the spinal cord to fill a linked sequence of reservoirs, called ventricles, that runs along the brain's central axis; by so doing, he makes the ventricles serve as liquid-filled shock absorbers.

The brain needs defenses against blood-borne bacteria and viruses; so, Harold lines the insides of brain capillaries with specialized endothelial cells that are tightly cemented together so as to repel pathogens. This assemblage of cells is called the blood-brain barrier. In order to allow critical molecular messengers to pass between the bloodstream and the brain, in some places, the blood-brain barrier is temporarily lowered by glial cells.

§

Only after having taken the steps that were described in the preceding paragraphs is Harold ready to create the cerebrum. The cerebrum contains billions of neurons, most of which connect exclusively with other neurons in the cerebrum. Much of this neuron-to-neuron connectivity is mediated by the corpus callosum, a large C-shaped nerve bundle that passes information back and forth between the two cerebral hemispheres.

Harold drapes the cerebrum over the subcortical brain, which comprises the sequence of nested neural shells that were described in a preceding paragraph; by virtue of surrounding them, the cerebrum joins the sequence and effectively becomes the outermost.

The cerebrum is a stratified structure, most of whose somas are located in its outermost layer; this layer is called the cerebral cortex. The rest of the cerebrum consists mostly of myelinated axons that connect the cerebral cortex to itself and to remote locations in the brain; this region is called the cerebral medulla.

(Strictly speaking, only mammals possess a cerebral cortex; the analogous structure in lower vertebrates is called the pallium. In the interest of simplicity, we'll disregard the pallium.)

The cortex, itself, is divided into sublayers, which may be as few as three and as many as six in number, depending upon which part of the medulla they overlie.

The cerebral cortex is so extensive and proves to be so useful that Harold increasingly places new neural structures within it; so much so that, one day, he discovers that he's filled it completely. After scratching his head for a while, Harold realizes that he can increase the capacity of the cortex simply by wrinkling the cerebrum. So, that's what he does. Over time, by repeatedly resorting to this expedient, Harold transforms the cerebrum into a patchwork of hills and valleys. (A hill is called a gyrus and a valley, a sulcus.) He employs the same technique in order to increase the capacity of the outermost layer of the cerebellum, which is called the cerebellar cortex.

Eventually, the space that's occupied by the subcortical brain likewise becomes completely filled. (In humans, the subcortical brain has about four times as many neurons as the cerebrum.) But unlike the cerebrum, the subcortical brain (except for the cerebellum) isn't susceptible to being wrinkled. The lack of additional space is problematic because, as his prototypes get bigger and more complex, Harold has to massively interconnect the axial nuclei. Such connections take up a lot of space.

He solves this problem by allocating real estate on parts of the cerebrum that lie near the brain's central axis and housing the desired interconnections therein. Such regions include the insula, parts of the cingulate, and parts of the frontal and temporal lobes.

By virtue of all of the preceding, the innermost shell of the vertebrate brain will come to contain the smallest, most ancient, most essential, most tightly integrated, and least energy-consuming components, while the outermost will come to contain the largest, most recent, least essential, least tightly coupled, and most energy-consuming. By way of example, if the cerebral cortex fails to develop or is deliberately excised, the brain's owner probably will continue to live; but if the axial nuclei are fatally injured or are deliberately removed, the owner will die.

ξ

By creating the cerebral cortex, Harold has set the stage for the emergence of highly complex behaviors, such as social living, intelligence, language, and rational thinking; but before information from the outside world can get to the cortex, it must pass through the neural shells that lie beneath the cerebrum. Because these shells are more ancient than the cortex, and because it was, in the past, these very shells that made all decisions, rational thinking will necessarily be grounded in primitive cognitive mechanisms, such as feelings, emotions, and instincts.

In particular, feelings will come to be essential to rational decision-making. For instance, whenever the brain needs to choose one option among several, it examines the choices, one at a time, and stops when an axial nucleus called the amygdala signals its approval. The amygdala accomplishes this by generating a feeling that's epitomized by the word, "Aha!" This tells the brain that the option that it's currently contemplating is the right one. Absent this feeling, the brain can't make a choice.

The amygdala's go-ahead is contingent upon an immediately preceding go-ahead having been generated by the enteric nervous system, a cognitive network that's embedded in the digestive tract. (So large and complex is the enteric nervous system that it's sometimes said to be a semi-independent brain.) The enteric nervous system's go-ahead is a manifestation of what's commonly called a "gut feeling."

This combination of rational thinking with irrational feeling generally will work well, but it will have a downside: if the brain's owner is angry or afraid, the brain will be likely to ignore options that are rational and reasonable, and, instead, embrace choices that are driven by the passions.

ξ

A sensory array is a two-dimensional matrix of neurons that are specialized for detecting a particular kind of stimulus. Externally oriented arrays detect sensations such as sights, scents, or sounds; internally oriented arrays detect sensations such as hunger, thirst, or nausea. The state of each neuron in a sensory array will be called a pixel, the joint states of all of the neurons will be called an image, and the internal or external reality that the image depicts will be called a scene.

A good artisan knows that simplifying things, especially reducing the number of redundant elements, is the key to robustness. But as Harold's prototypes get bigger and more complex, he has to increase the number of neurons in their sensory arrays; consequently, their brains are receiving an increasing number of signals, each of which conveys only one pixel's worth of information. If Harold doesn't do something soon, eventually the brains of his prototypes will be overwhelmed by a tidal wave of input.

Because primates, in order to survive, rely mainly upon the evidence of their eyes, the technique that Harold uses to forestall this catastrophe is best illustrated by the sense of sight.

ξ

The sensory array that supports vision is the retina. Whenever the retina acquires an interesting image, the brain selects an innate multilevel neural pyramid. The base of this pyramid is a two-dimensional array of neurons that lies within the primary visual cortex. Each member of this array receives signals from a corresponding set of retinal photoreceptors; consequently, the array in toto contains a nearly verbatim copy of the image on the retina.

Because this array constitutes the lowest level of the neural pyramid, it's designated as level 1. Via the axons that connect level 1 to level 2, the brain encodes, in the dendritic synapses of level 2, a representation of the image in level 1. (The configuration of such a synapse is altered, more or less permanently, by the stimulation that it receives from the neurons in level 1.)

Due to the fact that level 1 contains more neurons than level 2, the representation in the latter is likely to be smaller than the one in the former, and, if so, embodies a less accurate imitation of the original (the image on the retina.)

The image representation continues to be transmitted up the pyramid, one level at a time, progressively being reduced in size. At various levels, significant features of the image are identified and utilized to improve the representation.

But the brain has little interest in the image, itself; it's interested in the entities that it depicts. So, as the image representation is ascending the pyramid, at various levels, extraneous details are discarded so that, eventually, the representation encodes only one of the entities; the one that's most significant to the owner of the brain. Such an entity is called a referent; the refined image that represents it is called an object; and the pyramid in which the object is constructed is called an object pyramid. (Occasionally, I'll call it a sensory pyramid, instead.)

The encoded image of the referent can't undergo shrinking indefinitely; at some level, the reduction process ceases. The states of the dendritic synapses within this level jointly constitute the smallest possible representation of the referent that's faithful to the original. (We'll call such a representation a minimal facsimile.)

§

Unlike a geometric pyramid, which has only one apex, an object pyramid has several, [13] each of which is embodied in a single neuron. (Such neurons collectively are called apex neurons.)

1. *The request neuron* receives requests from remote parts of the brain to reconstruct the corresponding object.

2. *The response neuron* informs remote parts of the brain that the object has been reconstructed.

3. *The identification neuron* transmits a code that represents a referent that's being objectified.

4. *The recognition neuron* receives codes that represent unrecognized referents.

A signal that's received by the request neuron, or transmitted by the response neuron, can consist of as little as one voltage spike. Such a signal conveys no information, other than to acknowledge that some other part of the brain has an interest in the referent. We'll call such a signal a flag.

In contrast, a signal that's received by the recognition neuron, or transmitted by the identification neuron, comprises a sequence of many voltage spikes. Such a signal encodes information that was assembled by some other part of the brain.

A code-bearing signal can serve as a flag; but a flag can't serve as a code-bearing signal.

§

In order for an object pyramid to exchange information with other neural structures, consecutive levels of the pyramid are connected in such a way as to enable signals to pass not only upward toward the apexes, but also downward toward the base.

Whenever a request neuron is activated, it launches a cascade of neural signals, downward through the corresponding pyramid, that reconstructs a pixel image of the external scene from which the object was created, and deposits it in the base of the pyramid. (A computer performs a similar procedure whenever it needs to re-display a graphical image. This will be explained in Chapter 8.)

The reinstatement of the image sets off an upward cascade that entirely reconstructs the object. This causes the brain's owner momentarily to see the referent, which, in turn, enables the former to think about the latter.

For each externally oriented sense modality, including vision, olfaction, and hearing, Harold endows the brain with many neural pyramids, all of which share a common base that sequesters images from the corresponding sensory array. Whenever the array acquires an image that depicts a significant referent, the brain selects an unused pyramid and utilizes it to assemble a corresponding object. It then brings the referent to the attention of other parts of the brain, not via the many axons of the sensory array, but rather via the single axon of the response neuron. By this means, Harold forestalls the tidal wave of input that threatened to overwhelm the brain.

Sensory pyramids prove to be so useful that, over time, Harold makes more of them. But such structures consume large amounts of neural real estate; the only territory that can accommodate them is the cerebral cortex; so, this is where he puts them.

§

As Harold's prototypes get bigger, they attract the attention of formidable predators. In order to elude such monsters, the prototypes need to be able to recognize them quickly; but their vision systems can only produce images that are small and fuzzy.

Consequently, Harold decides to upgrade the vision system of his latest prototype by dramatically increasing the number of photoreceptors in its retina. This necessitates a commensurate increase in the size of its visual object pyramids; the high-resolution images that they make possible are essential to social living, intelligence, language, and rational thinking.

§

Increasingly, the axial nuclei are reacting to distinct external referents rather than to raw sensory images. The most important of these referents are the animal's conspecifics, to whom the axial nuclei jointly have begun to act as a counterpart during social transactions. In other words, the axial nuclei have begun to serve as a proxy for their owner; in so doing, they're becoming a neural self.

§

Objectification has become so essential to survival that Harold decides that nothing will be allowed to interfere with the construction of an object. Why? Because whenever a crisis arises, an object that's in the process of being constructed may be critical to handling that very crisis. So, he compels sensory arrays to send critical details of the images that they bear to centers of control, such as the axial nuclei, that can manage vital aspects of the body's response to an emergency, even while the corresponding objects are being assembled.

For instance, suppose that a bird flies straight toward the face of Harold's prototype. As the bird is approaching, information from the prototype's retina is passed to an axial nucleus called the superior colliculus, which utilizes this data to signal muscles that control the movement of the eyes. This enables the brain's owner to follow the rapidly approaching referent and evade it by ducking, even before it has objectified it and identified it as a bird.

§

Over the course of many more millions of years, Harold continues to refine his prototypes. Eventually, he produces an animal whose brain can construct so many objects of such high levels of detail that, within a few generations, it learns to hunt animals by following their footprints, use fire for warmth and cooking, and speak.

Harold has attained his goal; he's built a human being that has a human brain.

§

Before we leave Harold and his 650-million-year project, it's instructive to note that there has been no mention of consciousness, the mind, or qualia; nor has it been said that humans are the earth's dominant species or that there is one thing that distinguishes humans from all other animals.

Chapter 2: Neurons

It's generally known that a typical neuron comprises a cell body called a soma, a tree of short input projections called dendrites, and a long output projection called an axon. (An axon is sometimes called a nerve fiber.) Such a neuron is said to be multipolar. But there are many other configurations. For example, a bipolar neuron comprises a soma, a single dendrite, and an axon; a pseudounipolar neuron has a single projection that serves as a dendritic tree at one end and an axon at the other; and a unipolar brush cell has only dendrites, some of which transmit data to other neurons. For the most part, we'll consider only neurons that are multipolar or pseudounipolar.

Typically, a dendrite is thick, short, and tapered, whereas an axon is thin, long, and cylindrical.

Dendrites are studded with input portals that receive information from other neurons. In the interest of simplicity, we'll restrict our attention to one type of portal: a mushroom-shaped protuberance called a spine. If a spine is sufficiently stimulated by incoming signals, it generates an electrical impulse, which is modulated by the morphology of the dendrite to which the spine belongs. The dendrite consolidates the impulses from all of its spines and forwards the result to the soma.

In general, a spine receives input from only one neuron; such input typically is conveyed to the former via an axonal branch tip of the latter. The signal from a given neuron to a given spine is either always excitatory or always inhibitory; an excitatory signal increases, and an inhibitory signal decreases, the probability that the spine will discharge.

Spines can appear and disappear within hours and can change in size, shape, or conductivity within seconds; this changeability, which is called synaptic plasticity, undergirds learning. Plasticity that's associated with learning also occurs at the base of the axon.

A dendritic tree may comprise as many as 100 dendrites, each of which may have as many as 1,000 spines. This means that one neuron can consolidate signals from as many as 100,000 others.

Whenever a neuron's dendritic spines are competently stimulated, a region of the soma called the axon hillock, and a part of the axon called the axonal initial segment, cooperatively produce a sequence of voltages that courses rapidly down the length of the axon. This is called firing the axon. A sensory neuron can convey the intensity of a sensation by varying the number of voltages that it produces within a given time interval. (In other words, by increasing or decreasing their frequency.)

A voltage is also called an action potential or a voltage spike. Voltage sequences occur not only in neurons, but also in muscle fibers and endocrine cells.

The axon typically subdivides into many branches and has many output portals via which it can send signals to other cells. There are four kinds of such portals: intrinsic ports (protein-lined pores in the side of the axon,) gap junctions, varicosities, and branch tips. When the train of voltages reaches a portal, the portal reacts by secreting molecules either into another cell, or into an interstitial space, or into a capillary. [14] If it secretes into an interstitial space, the portal is said to be axo-extracellular; if into a capillary, it's said to be axo-secretory.

In some types of neurons, a sequence of voltages propagates not only forward, toward the distal ends of the axon, but also backward, toward the dendritic tree. What purpose this serves is as yet unknown, but one theory proposes that it plays a role in learning.

ξ

A neuron can pass a signal to another cell by electrical transmission, electrical induction, or chemical diffusion.

In electrical transmission, the firing of the axon causes electrically charged molecules (ions) and small uncharged molecules to pass from the axon directly into the target cell; this passage is facilitated by adjacent pores that are embedded in the cellular membranes of the two cells. Such an interface is called an electrical synapse. The matching pores jointly constitute a structure called a gap junction. A gap junction can change shape in order to alter the rate of flow of the molecules that pass through it. Gap junctions occur, not only in neurons, but also in many other kinds of cells. (Muscle fibers of the heart, for instance.)

In inductive transmission, if the axons of two neurons abut each other along their lengths, a sequence of voltages in one can electrically induce a like sequence in the other. This is called ephaptic coupling. Ephaptically coupled axons that are oriented in the same direction can synchronize events downstream. However, synchronization is more commonly achieved via gap junctions, especially if the cells that are to act in synchrony are many.

In chemical diffusion, whenever the axon fires, an ensemble of molecules, commonly called neurotransmitters or neuromodulators, is secreted through each intrinsic port, varicosity, or branch tip into a fluid-filled space. If this space is small, the axon releases a few molecules; if not, it releases many. In the former case, the secretions diffuse across the space and affect a single cell; in the latter, they float off and affect many. Often, these targets are neurons; but sometimes they're not.

For example, in order to cause a skeletal muscle fiber to contract, a motor neuron (also called a motoneuron) secretes acetylcholine onto a component of the fiber that's called a motor end plate. By this means, one motor neuron can innervate as few as 10 and as many as 1,000 muscle fibers, the average number being 150.

If the fluid-filled space (into which an axon secretes neuroactive molecules) is small, it's called a synaptic cleft; and the space and the transmitting and receiving molecular structures on the cell membranes jointly are called a chemical synapse. (The chemical synapse between a motor neuron and a motor end plate is called a neuromuscular junction.) A typical chemical synapse forwards a presynaptic signal to only one cell.

Typically, the receiving structure of a chemical synapse is located on the surface of a dendritic spine. The level of intensity (of the incoming stimulus) above which the spine will discharge is called its threshold. The threshold can vary depending on how often the spine is discharged; if frequently, the threshold is lowered; if infrequently, it's raised. It's likely that such changes are facilitated by glial cells that surround the synapse.

Another way of expressing that the threshold has been lowered is to say that the synapse has been strengthened. Like synaptic plasticity, which was described in a preceding paragraph, synaptic strengthening undergirds learning.

If neurotransmitters are conveyed to another cell by passing out of an intrinsic port or by leaking inadvertently out of a synapse, the transmission is called non-synaptic.

If an axonal branch tip of one neuron forms a chemical synapse with a dendritic spine of another, the former can pass a signal to the latter. (An axonal branch tip is also called an axon terminal, a presynaptic terminal, a terminal bouton, a synaptic bouton, a synaptic knob, or a synaptic end-foot; but I'll refrain from using these other terms.) The neuron that provides the axonal branch tip is called presynaptic, the one that provides the dendritic spine is called postsynaptic, and the synapse is said to be axo-dendritic.

However, this isn't the only way by which a chemical signal can be passed from one neuron to another; just about any major component (dendrite, soma, or axon) of one neuron can form a chemical synapse with any component of another. So, a chemical synapse may be either axo-dendritic, axo-somatic, or axo-axonal; or somato-dendritic or somato-somatic; or dendro-dendritic or dendro-axonal. (Some of these names more commonly are spelled without a hyphen.)

If the presynaptic and postsynaptic neurons of a chemical synapse are one and the same, the synapse is called an autapse. It's possible that an autapse enables the neuron of which it's a part to accumulate consecutive self-generated signals and, when a predetermined threshold has been reached, dispatch a signal to another cell. By this means, the neuron can act as a counter or a timer; successful communication with the other cell discharges the accumulated signal and effectively resets the counter or timer to zero.

In general, a neuron secretes neuroactive molecules only from its axon; but a magnocellular neuron of the hypothalamus also can secrete such molecules from its dendrites. Usually, an axon secretes identical molecules through all of its portals; but recently, neurons in the midbrain have been alleged to secrete dopamine through one set of portals and glutamate through another.

Some kinds of neurons (amacrine cells of the retina, for instance) have both electrical and chemical synapses.

§

Whenever a secreted molecule binds to an appropriate receptor, it rearranges the electrostatic forces around the binding site, causing the receptor to change shape. This is analogous to a mailman opening a mailbox in order to deliver a letter. So, in my opinion, it's more sensible to conceive of such a molecule as a messenger, rather than as a message.

A secretory cell is well suited for distributing molecular messengers widely but indiscriminately (by utilizing the bloodstream.) In contrast, a neuron is well suited for delivering such messengers to particular locations with great specificity. However, neither mechanism is capable of rapidly distributing messengers to billions of specific locations concurrently; but that's precisely what needs to happen if many parts of the brain must react in a simultaneous and coordinated manner.

What's needed is a mechanism by which a single neuron can broadcast a signal widely; so, some types of neurons have very long axons that secrete molecular messengers through thousands of portals.

For instance, within a human, a relatively small cluster in the pons called the locus coeruleus contains 10,000 neurons, each of which transports norepinephrine to as many as 250,000 other neurons; [15] that is to say, the locus coeruleus is capable of applying norepinephrine to 2.5 billion neurons simultaneously. (This constitutes 3% of the neurons in the cranial brain.) The locus coeruleus is instrumental in the fear cascade: a body-wide sequence of actions that's launched by the hypothalamus in order to prepare the brain and the body for fight or flight.

An alternative name for norepinephrine is noradrenaline; an alternative name for a related molecule, epinephrine, is adrenaline. The British pharmacopoeia uses the word, "adrenaline," rather than the word, "epinephrine."

Neurons

Neurons aren't the only kind of brain cells that transmit electrochemical signals: so do astrocytes. (They communicate with one another via gap junctions.) An astrocyte is a glial cell that can envelop as many as 2,000,000 chemical synapses and regulate their operations. For the most part, in the interest of brevity, we won't consider glial cells.

§

Notwithstanding the many similarities between brains and computers, their differences are significant. In particular, a computer can halt the execution of its current set of instructions, launch the execution of a second set, and, when the execution of the second has terminated, resume the execution of the first; the brain, on the other hand, because of the properties of neurons, cannot suspend a neural process and subsequently continue where it left off.

Chapter 3: The Axial Nuclei

In order to visualize where, in a human, particular axial nuclei are located, you need to know the major divisions of the human brain. From uppermost to lowermost, they are the cerebrum, the basal ganglia, the midbrain, the pons, and the medulla oblongata. Together, the pons and the medulla oblongata are called the brainstem. For the purpose of understanding behavior, it's useful to regard the spinal cord and the enteric nervous system as components of the brain, too.

There's an additional structure called the cerebellum that's attached to the rear of the pons. The principal task of the cerebellum is to smooth out the operation of complex processes. In particular, it integrates inputs from the brain and the spinal cord in order to fine-tune bodily motion. Its corrugated outer surface is called the cerebellar cortex. For the most part, in the interest of brevity, we'll disregard the cerebellum.

The largest component of the cranial brain is the cerebrum. The cerebrum is divided into two hemispheres, a left and a right, which, themselves, are divided into four lobes: the frontal, the temporal, the parietal, and the occipital. (Two others, the limbic and insular lobes, are less frequently referred to. The insular lobe also is known as the insular cortex or the insula.)

Overall, the structure of the cerebrum is similar to that of a citrus fruit, with the cerebral cortex serving as the rind and the cerebral medulla serving as the pith. For the most part, our interest will be in the rind rather than the pith.

The cerebrum is draped over the basal ganglia, the midbrain, the pons, the medulla oblongata, and the cerebellum. This assemblage and its interconnections will be called the subcortical brain. The subcortical brain, together with the cerebrum, constitute a sequence of nested neural shells (of which the cerebrum is the outermost) that make up the cranial brain.

Most of the axial nuclei reside in the subcortical brain, but some reside in the cerebrum. The hippocampus, for instance, is located in the medial temporal lobe of the cerebrum. Because a nucleus generally is conceived as a cluster of cells, the layered structure of the hippocampus would seem to indicate that it's a cortex rather than a nucleus. But the hippocampus has a convoluted three-dimensional shape that swirls together different kinds of layers. In the interest of simplicity, and for the purpose of understanding behavior, it's more useful to conceive of such a cortex-like assemblage as a nucleus.

Running through the middle of the cranial brain, from the medulla oblongata to the cerebral cortex, is a loose network of 100 axial nuclei that jointly are called the reticular formation; one of its structures, the ascending reticular activating system, regulates wakefulness and sleep-wake transitions.

In order to forestall confusion, I need to alert you to the fact that, although most nuclei come in pairs, a left and a right, it's customary to refer to them by using the singular form of their names. In general, the plural form is used only if there are more than two of them.

Also, some structures, such as the thalamus and the hypothalamus, that routinely are called nuclei are actually clusters of nuclei.

§

The human brain contains hundreds of nuclei. Because nuclei are the most important components of the nervous system, and because the axial nuclei are the most important of all, I'm going to list seven of the latter and describe their major functions:

- The thalamus mediates much of the communication between the subcortical brain and the cerebral cortex. It's mainly known as a hub for the transmission of sensory data in all modalities (olfactory signals go to the cerebrum first and thence to the thalamus); but it also transmits motor signals and plays a role in arousal, attention, and awareness. The thalamus is located at the center of the brain. It's tightly integrated with the basal ganglia, which roughly form a sphere around the thalamus. In the interest of simplicity, we'll consider the thalamus to be a part of the basal ganglia.

The thalamus includes the pulvinar, which controls visual attention and visual saccades, and the lateral geniculate nucleus, which performs diverse low-level operations on signals from the retina and integrates visual information with auditory information.

- The hypothalamus performs so many regulatory tasks that it can be thought of as a primordial brain; in conjunction with its junior partner, the pituitary, it links the nervous system to the endocrine system and thereby maintains homeostasis. Among its responsibilities are the management of body temperature, blood pressure, hunger, thirst, fatigue, sleep, circadian rhythms, parenting, social attachment, and the fear cascade, which galvanizes the brain and the body so that they can deal with a mortal danger. The hypothalamus is located in front of and slightly below the thalamus.

  The hypothalamus includes the suprachiasmatic nucleus, which participates in the control of circadian rhythms, the paraventricular nucleus, which reacts to changes in the body and manages the body's response to stress, and the supraoptic nucleus, which manages water absorption in the kidneys.

- The pituitary (which also is known as the hypophysis) acts as a junior partner to the hypothalamus in maintaining homeostasis. In particular, it helps in controlling growth, blood pressure, metabolism, temperature, pregnancy, childbirth, and nursing. The pituitary is located just below the hypothalamus.

- The superior colliculus influences attention and generates spatially directed eye movements, head turns, and arm-reaching movements. The superior colliculus is located on the rear of the midbrain.

- The hippocampus plays important roles in memory consolidation, spatial memory, and spatial navigation. The hippocampus curls around the bottom of the thalamus and terminates in the amygdala.

- The amygdala participates in decision-making, emotional response, and memory processing. The amygdala is located at the front end of the hippocampus near the lower part of the side of the thalamus.

- The locus coeruleus affects arousal, sleep-wake cycles, attention, memory, and balance. Loss of neurons in the locus coeruleus has been linked to posttraumatic stress disorder (PTSD.) The locus coeruleus is located in the pons.

§

In order to understand human behavior, it's useful to appreciate to what extent essential life processes are managed via secretion. So, here's a list of 14 of the body's most important molecular messengers, the main nuclei, glands, and organs that secrete them, and the major functions that they serve. (The first six of the messengers in the list are secreted by the pituitary.)

- Melanocyte-stimulating hormone stimulates the production and release of melanin and plays a role in sexual arousal. Melanin is widely known as a pigment that affects skin color; but its many variants serve other functions as well.

- Thyroid-stimulating hormone controls metabolism via the thyroid gland.

- Follicle-stimulating hormone regulates reproduction and the maturation that occurs during puberty.

- Growth hormone stimulates the growth of all internal organs except the brain; increases calcium retention, bone mineralization, muscle mass, and protein synthesis; reduces liver uptake of glucose; maintains pancreatic islet cells; and stimulates the immune system.

- Adrenocoricotropic hormone influences circadian rhythms and responds to stress by stimulating the production and release of cortisol.

- Prolactin stimulates maternal behavior, particularly milk production; controls the development of a fetus's neurons, lungs, and immune system; regulates the interactions between the fetus's immune system and its mother's; and stimulates the production of myelin. Myelin is a whitish fatty substance that surrounds and electrically insulates the axons of most types of neurons.

- Vasopressin is secreted by the pituitary and by the supraoptic nucleus of the hypothalamus. Vasopressin regulates blood pressure and urination and plays a role in social behavior, pair bonding, sexual motivation, and maternal responses to stress.

- Oxytocin is secreted by the supraoptic and paraventricular nuclei of the hypothalamus; it plays a significant role in social bonding, including coitus, orgasm, childbirth, maternal behavior, breastfeeding, pair bonding, anxiety, and social recognition.

- Histamine is secreted by the tuberomammillary nucleus of the hypothalamus. However, it's also secreted by the stomach and by mast cells that are located in the connective tissue of the skeletal system at sites of potential injury. Histamine is involved in the inflammatory response of the immune system and contributes to arousal and sleep-wake processing.

- Dopamine is secreted by the substantia nigra, a part of the ascending reticular activating system that's located in the midbrain. Dopamine plays an important role in motor control; loss of dopaminergic neurons in the substantia nigra causes Parkinson's disease. Dopamine also affects motivation, arousal, reinforcement, reward, sexual gratification, milk production, and nausea. Dopamine is both a neurotransmitter and a hormone.

- Serotonin is secreted by cells within the enteric nervous system, and by the Raphe nuclei, components of the ascending reticular activating system that are located in the brainstem. Serotonin is involved in pain inhibition, emotion, and mood regulation.

- Glutamate is the main excitatory neurotransmitter of the vertebrate nervous system. It's also secreted by cells within the liver and the kidneys. Glutamate is an amino acid.

- Acetylcholine is secreted by motor neurons into the neuromuscular junctions that activate the muscles. It also is secreted by neurons in the brain and the autonomic nervous system.

- Norepinephrine is secreted by the locus coeruleus, a part of the ascending reticular activating system that's located in the pons. Norepinephrine is both a neurotransmitter and a hormone.

Three-quarters of the functions in the preceding list influence sex-related behaviors.

All told, nuclei in the brain, and glands and organs in the body, secrete as many as 200 kinds of molecular messengers into cells, interstitial spaces, and the bloodstream.

§

Having completed these three initial chapters, we now are ready to conduct a systematic investigation of behavior; it begins by singling out the most fundamental activity of life, the conversion of sensation into motion, and identifying the smallest biological entities that can perform it.

Chapter 4: What is Life?

It's easier to define life by specifying what living things do, rather than by specifying what they are. Anything that's alive:

1.   Transforms sensation into motion. [16]

2.   Systematically obtains raw materials from the environment.

3.   Constructs a self.

4.   Procreates.

5.   Cycles continually between eating, avoiding being eaten, and reproducing. [17]

Although procreation widely is believed to be the most fundamental property of life, it could not have evolved into constructing a self, transforming sensation into motion, importing raw materials from the environment, and switching bodily context. Instead, it was the converting of sensation into motion that gave rise to the others. [18] (The significance of transforming sensation into motion is explained by Rodolfo Llinás in his book, "i of the vortex.")

In order to maintain itself, a living cell needs many different kinds of molecular machines. Of all known types of biomolecules, only proteins are sufficiently diverse to serve in this capacity.

A protein is an ordered sequence of amino acids. An amino acid is a small carbon-based molecule that's made up of two components: one that enables all types of amino acids to link together in chains of arbitrary length, and another that enables each type to perform a specific chemical function. A typical human cell contains 20,000 types of proteins, which, altogether, amount to 2 billion proteins per cell.

A protein performs its designated function by assuming a particular shape that's characteristic of that type of protein. (The electrostatic bonds that link together a protein's amino acids are just strong enough to hold the protein together while allowing it to bend.) It achieves this shape by passing through four stages of construction:

- The primary structure of a protein is a sequence of amino acids that's assembled by a molecular machine called a ribosome. A ribosome connects the amino acids, one to another, according to a molecular transcript that's derived from the human genome.

- The secondary structure is a sequence of spikey spirals and pleated sheets, interspersed with unmodified lengths of the primary structure; it's the result of a rapid spontaneous cascade of hydrogen bonding between components of the amino acid chain. (A hydrogen bond is an electrostatic link between a hydrogen atom of one molecule and a more electronegative atom, such as nitrogen or oxygen, of another. Transient shifts in electron density within atoms and molecules also contribute to hydrogen bonding.)

- The tertiary structure is a three-dimensional shape that results from the aggregation of amino acids in the secondary structure by virtue of their mutual affinity or antipathy for water, with hydrophobic groups tending to bury themselves in the inside of the structure and hydrophilic groups tending to cluster on the outside. The tertiary structure may further be consolidated by the binding of pairs of cysteine molecules. A cysteine molecule is a type of amino acid; a link between two cysteine molecules is called a disulfide bridge.

- The quaternary structure is the overall globular or elongated shape of the protein. It's the result of bonding between tertiary subunits, which, themselves, may have bonded with other kinds of molecules.

A hemoglobin molecule, for instance, is a spherical quaternary structure that's comprised of four tertiary subunits. Each subunit is attached to a heme functional group that can bind, and subsequently release, one molecule of oxygen. Because the active site of a heme group contains an iron atom, hemoglobin is classed as a metalloprotein.

Most proteins spontaneously fold into the correct shape; but some require the help of special molecules called chaperones. The overall shape of a protein may further be altered by the electrostatic influence of molecules that come into close proximity with the protein, and by the buffeting to which the protein is subjected by the nano-scale, thermodynamic, molecular storm that constantly rages within the cell; in other words, by heat. [19]

The amino acid chain that constitutes a protein is assembled by a molecular machine called a ribosome. A mammalian cell may contain as many as 10,000,000 ribosomes, each of which can assemble a protein in less than 10 seconds. Often, after a ribosome has put together a protein, other molecular machines make adjustments to its shape; if the protein is to be transported elsewhere, they also may append a lipid or a carbohydrate that indicates its destination.

Protein structures are too small to be seen directly, but the shape of a particular kind can be deduced by condensing a large number of them into a crystal, bombarding the crystal with x-rays, and observing the pattern that's formed as the crystalline lattice scatters the rays. This is how it was determined that a hemoglobin molecule is roughly spherical.

If a protein were to be viewed from a short distance away, it would look like an irregular pockmarked solid. [20] If the shape of the space within such a pockmark happens to match sufficiently well the shape of a protrusion on the surface of some other molecule, then the molecule can dock with the protein by filling this space; that is to say, by pushing the protrusion into the pockmark. (There are other ways by which a protein can conjoin with a molecule.) Whenever this happens, a redistribution of electrostatic forces around the docking site causes the protein to change shape.

The acceptance by the protein of the molecule is tantamount to sensation, and the shape change thus induced is tantamount to motion; in other words, a protein is capable of performing the most fundamental activity of life: the transformation of sensation into movement. [21]

That the docking of a molecule to a protein is tantamount to sensation is illustrated by the sense of smell. In mammals, the sense of smell is activated by the binding of an odorous molecule to a protein on the dendrite of a bipolar neuron in the nose. (These are the only neurons of the central nervous system that extend outside the body.) The binding of the odorant changes the shape of the binding site, which triggers a cascade of electrochemical reactions that transmits a signal to the olfactory bulb, and thence to the amygdala, the hippocampus, and various other locations in the brain.

ξ

A molecule that docks with a protein is called a substrate. Within such a protein, there's nothing to prevent a second docking site, that's located adjacent to the first, from capturing a second substrate, not necessarily of the same species as the first. If the combined shape changes of the two docking sites brings their corresponding substrates into close proximity, then the substrates, themselves, may bond together. Such bonding causes another local redistribution of electrostatic forces that can open the compound dock and release the newly synthesized molecule. This process is effectively a chemical reaction between the substrates, and the protein that performs it is effectively a chemical factory.

Typically, whenever such a protein releases its product, it returns to the shape that it had before the substrates docked with it. If this is the case, then it's said to be an enzyme. However, an enzyme may contain more than one protein. [22] It also may contain ribonucleic acid (RNA); in fact, an enzyme may consist only of RNA. An enzyme can turn out a product as frequently as 600,000 times per second. [23]

Besides joining a substrate to some other molecule, a protein can transform it in other ways. It may divide the substrate into smaller molecules, or alter its charge, or change its shape. (In the latter case, if the substrate is, itself, a protein, then the bonding protein may alter the function that the substrate protein theretofore had been performing.) When the bonding protein has finished its work, it releases the resulting products. A product may then go on to bond to another protein and undergo a further transformation. Such transforming proteins are effectively molecular machines, and a series of such machines can form what's effectively an assembly line. [24]

In addition to serving as fabricating machines, production lines, and molecular factories, proteins can serve as motors, pumps, impellers, transporters, storage repositories, structural elements, pathways, messengers, dispatchers, receivers, switches, transducers, amplifiers, adapters, clocks, and germ killers. [25-26]

This versatility affords to the cell a way to reproduce, import food and atmospheric gasses, and maintain a dynamic and ongoing balance between its internal constituents; the latter process, which is called cellular homeostasis, is the substrate upon which the construction of the self, and the transitions between violence, sex, and work, are built. Together with the transformation of sensation into motion, these constitute the defining activities of life; that is to say, all five of life's fundamental behaviors can be conducted by cooperating protein structures.

Molecular machines and molecular factories can operate if they're immersed in a fluid whose temperature is conducive to life; an ocean, for instance. However, life can't occur unless such molecules are enclosed by a membrane (specifically, by the circumferential membrane of a cell.) [27] But how does an enclosing membrane promote life?

When viewed from the outside, a cell looks like a serene being that's peaceably pulsing with life; but when viewed from the inside, it looks more like a bag, filled mostly with water, whose contents are briskly and continually moving. [28-29] This turbulence guarantees that every free molecule will visit every part of the cell at least once per second, [30] and that if two molecules can react with each other, eventually they will. [31]

The large number of molecules that are inside the cell, [32] their smallness, their close confinement by the cell membrane, the high intensity of their electrostatic fields, operating across such minute distances, [33] the water molecules that surround, lubricate, and protonate them, [34] the virtual absence of gravity, [35] the buffeting to which they are subjected by the ceaseless molecular storm, and the laws of chance ensure that the right substrates dock with the right proteins with sufficient frequency to promote life.

Throughout our galaxy's 13.6-billion-year history, in oceans on various planets and moons, lipid membranes (double sheets of fat molecules) spontaneously engulfed proteins, and with them, various other kinds of molecules. Such encapsulations, conducted a prodigious number of times, in a prodigious number of places, on a large number of moons and planets, over such a large span of time, probably made it inevitable that such a capsule would one day exhibit the five fundamental behaviors of life, and thereby earn the right to be called a living being. Thenceforth, its descendants could have spread throughout the galaxy on the ejecta of colliding planetary bodies. Among them, there may have been one who, by being refined via evolution and natural selection, became the progenitor of all earthly life.

Chapter 5: The Conversion of Sensation into Motion

If the concepts of sensation and motion are broadened a little, they can be applied to the study of biology at all levels; from the intricate activities of cells to the large-scale dynamics of crowds. For instance, the binding of a molecule to a protein can trigger a redistribution of electrostatic forces that changes the shape of the protein. The binding of the molecule is tantamount to sensation, and the shape change thus induced is tantamount to motion. Via this mechanism, proteins manage the processing of nucleic acids, minerals, carbohydrates, and lipids, as well as the conversion of energy from one form to another.

It isn't only proteins that transform sensation into motion: so do viruses (when they're inside a cell,) nucleic acids, archaea, and bacteria; on a higher level, so do tissues, glands, organs, and muscles; an on an even higher level, so do protists, fungi, plants, and animals.

In animals, the transformation of sensation into motion undergirds embryonic development, homeostasis, and reflexes; in social animals, it underlies social behavior; and in humans, it underprops speech. (During a conversation, each interlocutor transforms auditory sensations into movement of the diaphragm, lungs, vocal cords, mouth, and tongue.)

One instance of transforming sensation into motion is called a decision odyssey. A decision odyssey is a virtual voyage that originates as sensation, passes through the body, and emerges as motion. (One odyssey can comprise multiple concurrent or sequential sub-odysseys.) Within the context of this paradigm, a decision is the transition from sensing to moving; that is to say, it's whatever cognition takes place along the route via which the odyssey passes through the body.

Some decisions are deliberately attended and carefully thought out; but most decisions aren't. The execution of the patellar reflex is a good example. [36]

The patellar reflex is a type of stretch reflex. Stretch reflexes are one of 60 different kinds of reflexes that take place within the human body.

In order to do a quick test of a patient's nervous system, a doctor taps the lower quadriceps tendon, just below the kneecap (the patella) with a rubber hammer. The tap stretches the tendon, which stimulates 1,300 muscle spindles (stretch detectors) within the quadriceps muscle group.

What's called the patellar reflex is the decision odyssey that originates in any one of these muscle spindles. Each spindle sends a signal that traverses the dendritic-axonal projection of a pseudounipolar sensory neuron and crosses, via a synapse within the spinal cord, into a motor neuron. The signal courses down the motor neuron's axon to a group of motor end plates that are located within the same muscle as the spindle that sent the signal. Each end plate then triggers a contraction in a single muscle fiber.

By virtue of these multiple and simultaneous contractions, the entire muscle assemblage shortens, and, as a result, the leg kicks. The force of the contractions is influenced by the tension in other muscles and by the current state of the body.

The shortening of the quadriceps muscles is accompanied by a lengthening of the hamstring muscles. Whenever an animal decides to run, its brain commandeers many such reciprocal reflexes in order to coordinate muscular contractions and extensions throughout the body.

The execution of the patellar reflex is an observable decision odyssey. An observable odyssey is one in which the sensation and motion occur on the outside of the body, and, thus, are accessible to an observer; however, most decision odysseys aren't observable; [37] they start and end entirely inside the body, are mediated by its most anciently evolved centers of control, and typically are involuntary. (Homeostatic and digestive actions are good examples.) Nevertheless, highly disciplined individuals, such as Buddhist monks, can control some of their own internal decision odysseys deliberately.

In animals, translations of sensation into motion are mainly facilitated by the brain. [38] Over the course of evolutionary history, as Nature increased the size and complexity of animal bodies, it also increased the size and complexity of their brains; it accomplished this by incrementally accreting new layers of neurons that executed new kinds of decision odysseys. For the purpose of understanding behavior, such odysseys, regardless of whether they're conscious and deliberate, will be called cognition, and the strata that perform them will be called cognitive layers.

Vertebrate brains possess five such strata: [39]

1. The enteric nervous system is a cognitive layer that controls digestion and elimination. Unlike the remaining four layers, which reside within the cranium and the spinal cord, the enteric nervous system resides within the gastrointestinal tract of the body.

    Before the advent of the gastrointestinal tract, life-forms consumed their food by absorbing it; the tract, whose forwardmost component is the mouth, enabled creatures who were so equipped to consume their nutriment by eating it, instead. Although "eating" routinely is employed as a shorthand for "the intake of food by any kind of life-form," only animals truly eat.

2. The primordial core is a layer that regulates homeostasis, smooth bodily motion, and fixed action patterns. A feeling is a somatic fixed action pattern, a reflex is a neural fixed action pattern, and an emotion is a neural fixed action pattern that results in a feeling. [40]

    An emotion is initiated by the convergence of a set of inputs; many different such sets can trigger the same emotion; but the emotion always results in the divergence of a canonical set of outputs. The outputs, in turn, trigger the corresponding feeling.

    For instance, although the fear emotion can be triggered by diverse sets of sensations, it always results in the rapid cascade of a specific set of actions within the body. The many nuclei, glands, and organs that are affected by the fear cascade will be enumerated in Chapter 10.

    The primordial core emerged when Nature began to replace cellular homeostatic processes with bodily homeostatic decision odysseys. [41] Initially, such operations were managed by secretory control centers; later, many came to be managed by neuronal centers.

> Via the bloodstream and an assemblage of neurons, the primordial core partially controls the enteric nervous system.

3. The self shell is a layer that regulates deliberate activities that benefit only the brain's owner; its advent enabled the brain to conduct voluntary unitary actions.

4. The family shell is a layer that regulates activities that benefit the extended family group to which the owner of the brain belongs; its advent enabled the brain to conduct binary social transactions.

5. The imaging shell is a layer that objectifies complex sensory images; its advent enabled the brain to conduct intricate behaviors, such as social living, intelligence, language, and rational thinking.

§

Nerves that transmit sensations can't be connected arbitrarily to nerves that produce motions: [42] after some initial period of development or learning, inputs must bring about outputs that are appropriate in terms of survival. This means that sensation is translated into motion according to a template that's appropriate to the animal and to its environment. This template resides mostly in the brain, where it serves as a model of the real external world and of the body's place within that world.

In other words, in order for the transformation of sensation into motion to be meaningful, it must be filtered through a world model.

Chapter 6: The Brain as a World Model

When a wildebeest baby is born, it struggles to its feet; whenever its mother runs, it runs, too. [43] These instinctive behaviors strongly suggest that the baby's brain contains an innate world model. [44] The model informs the baby that the savannah is a dangerous place and that safety lies in sticking close to Mother.

It isn't surprising that the brain contains a world model; what's surprising is that the world model utilizes virtually all of the brain's neurons. At first glance, this notion would seem to contradict the fact that much of the brain is taken up with managing the body; but the resource that the brain employs to interact with the body is the same resource that it employs to interact with the outside world. This universal resource consists of topographic maps.

So, for example, a vertebrate's brain contains not only a map of its proprietary territory in the external world, but also maps of the limbs, muscles, bones, joints, organs, and epithelial surfaces in its body. [45]

In addition, its brain, in cooperation with the senses, creates maps of external referents; such a map is called a sensory image. In general, the brain transforms the map of an external referent into a neural artifact called an object; among the most important of these are objects that represent other animals.

In order to forestall overwhelming its owner with details, the brain merges all of these elements into a seamless, continuous vision of everything that's known to it. This internal model of the world, which is virtually coextensive with the brain, is the animal's chief resource for making decisions.

That the primary mission of the brain is to model the world so that it can change sensation into motion is an alternative to the traditional notion of mindedness: that there exists an entity, called the mind, that purposefully controls the body. This entity is said to inhabit a dimension that's separate from the physical reality that's occupied by the brain. Were this to be true, then it might be possible for the mind to survive the death of its owner and be imported into another biological or mechanical body, or be elevated into some metaphysical plane. The idea that the brain is predominantly a world model makes this notion superfluous [46] and enables ethology and psychology to be calibrated against evolution.

§

An animal parses the external world into discrete entities, relationships, and transactions. This implies that somewhere within its brain, along the paths that convert sensory input into muscular output, entities, relationships, and transactions are represented by neural artifacts.

There are two fundamental kinds of neural artifacts, objects and connections, from which all others are built. For example, an effector comprises two objects and one connection, and a transaction comprises two effectors.

These artifacts, together with a large suite of presumptions, constitute an animal's unique, private, internal understanding of the external world.

The internal representation of a discrete entity is called an object. An animal's most important object is the one that it references whenever it attends to its own body. This artifact is called the self object. The internal representation of an animal that's significant to the brain's owner is called an avatar. In order for an individual to interact with a conspecific, in addition to a self object, its brain must contain an avatar that represents the other party.

External entities are internalized by a process called objectification; [47] but the objectification process also internalizes relationships. [48] An internalized relationship is called a connection. A connection may be mono-directional or bidirectional. Two neural artifacts can be mono-directionally connected by a neural path that links a neuron within the first artifact to a designated neuron within the second; but for two artifacts to be bidirectionally connected, in addition, a similar path is needed that links a neuron within the second artifact to a neuron within the first. In order to forestall an infinite loop of signals, the first pair of neurons cannot be identical to the second.

Of all possible relationships, those that include the animal, itself, are the most significant and are internalized as connections between the self object and other artifacts. If the relationship is an interaction with another animal, it's internalized as a connection between the self object and an avatar that represents that animal. Such connections are called predicates. (However, I'll also use the word, "predicate," to denote a connection that conducts a neural signal within a reflex.)

Although it's possible for an animal to interact simultaneously with multiple partners, in general it interacts with only one at a time. Whenever it does so, the other protagonist usually reciprocates. Such an event pair is called a binary transaction, and each event is called a unitary action. Rarely does an encounter between two animals end directly after the first exchange; on the contrary, one transaction is followed by another, which, in turn, is followed by another, and so on.

A duel, for instance, may comprise hundreds of transactions, each of which is composed of an exchange of blows. Within such a sequence, sensory input to one combatant is transformed into muscular output that's directed against the other, who interprets it as sensory input and transforms it into muscular output that's directed against the former, and so on. (This is illustrated in Figure 2.)

Actions and transactions are carried out by dispositional representations. (The concept of a dispositional representation is explained by Antonio Damasio in his book, "Descartes' Error.")

A dispositional representation is an embodied executable program. [49] Unlike a computer program, whose instructions typically are copied from memory and executed in the central processing unit, a dispositional representation is executed in place. A social transaction, such as an exchange of blows, is conducted by a dispositional representation in the brain; a reflex, which may be conceived as an internal transaction, is conducted by a dispositional representation in the body

§

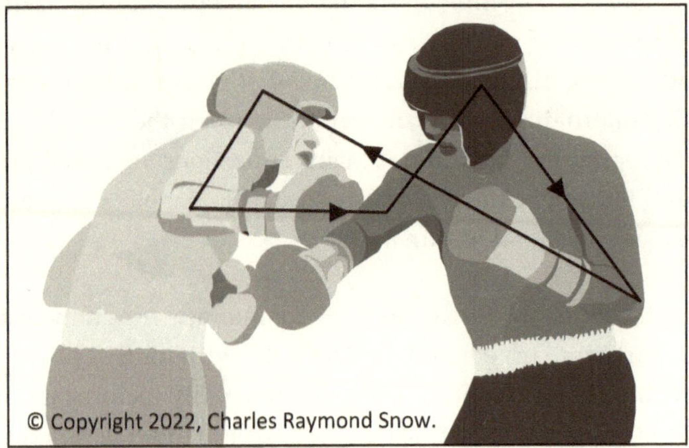

Figure 2: An Exchange of Blows is a Binary Transaction

In a boxing match, sensory input to one combatant is transformed into muscular output that's directed against the other, who interprets it as sensory input and transforms it into muscular output that's directed against the former, and so on.

A dispositional representation that executes a unitary action is called an effector. (Unfortunately, the word, "effector," also denotes a cell or an organ that acts in response to a stimulus; I won't make use of this denotation.)

If a unitary action is part of a social transaction, then the effector that represents it in the brain is instantiated by two neural artifacts, the first of which is connected mono-directionally to the second. The first artifact represents the initiator; the second represents the recipient; and the connection represents the action that the former performs upon the latter. The role of either the initiator or the recipient is fulfilled by the self object of the brain's owner; and the remaining role is fulfilled by an object that represents the other animal, who usually is a member of the owner's extended family.

If the owner of the brain is the recipient, the effector is said to be inbound and corresponds to an action that the other animal has just performed upon the owner. If the owner is the initiator, the effector is said to be outbound and corresponds to an action that the owner is about to perform upon the other animal.

Whenever an outbound effector is executed, control of the body is passed to an innate, learned, or ad hoc procedure that dispatches instructions to the muscles and the viscera.

Effectors always come in pairs, an inbound and an outbound; the inbound effector always is first; and the two are always linked together via the self object. An inbound effector linked to an outbound effector is called a transaction.

Because an object occupies a large amount of neural real estate, within an effector, it's represented by a much smaller artifact that acts as a pointer to that object. A pointer may be as simple as a single neuron that possesses two special connections: one to the corresponding object pyramid and another to the neuron's successor within the transaction.

(A protagonist of a social action is symbolized within an effector via two levels of representation: a pointer represents the corresponding object, and the object represents the protagonist. A similar recursion lies at the heart of topographic psychology; its principles constitute a de facto model of the brain, and the brain constitutes a de facto model of the world. In order to avoid having to say "a representation of a representation" or "a model of a model," we'll disregard such iterations.)

ς

An animal experiences its life as a series of encounters, each of which comprises a sequence of transactions between itself and others. In every such transaction, the second protagonist usually is a member of the animal's extended family; but sometimes, it's a member of some other family, or a friendly or contentious member of some other species, or a predator.

Within the brain of each participant, each transaction is represented by an ordered pair of effectors, the first of which is inbound and the second, outbound. Moreover, the two effectors are linked by virtue of the fact that the recipient of the first is one and the same as the initiator of the second; namely, the self object. This linkage enables the execution of the first effector to trigger the execution of the second. The brain may interject cognition between the inbound and outbound effectors; in the interest of brevity, we'll ignore this complication.

From the standpoint of each participant, the initiating deed of the first transaction corresponds to an action that the other animal has just performed upon the self, and the final deed of the last transaction corresponds to an action that the self is about to perform, in response, upon the other animal. Even if the response, as perceived by an observer, is for the animal that owns the self to do nothing, there is, nevertheless, muscular output that's calibrated to freeze it in its current position and stance.

ξ

Effectors that represent social actions are created in response to events that occur within the lifespan of the brain's owner; but there are other types that were created via natural selection during the phylogenetic history of the owner's species. Such effectors are assembled during the fetal development of the owner and are said to be innate. The protagonists of innate effectors are organs, glands, nuclei, neural somas, neurons, or neuron-like structures such as muscle spindles or motor end plates.

The patellar reflex, for instance, is implemented by a pair of innate effectors. [50] The initiator of the inbound effector is a spindle within the quadriceps muscle group, the predicate is the dendritic-axonal projection of a pseudounipolar sensory neuron, and the recipient is the soma, of a motor neuron, that resides within the spinal cord inside one of the lumbar vertebrae (vertebra L2, L3, or L4.) The initiator of the outbound effector is the soma of the motor neuron, the predicate is its axon, and the recipient is a group of motor end plates that reside within the same muscle as the spindle. Whenever the first effector is activated, it, in turn, activates the second; in both effectors, the action that's performed by the predicate is to convey a neural signal.

The patellar reflex can be conceived as a binary transaction between the quadriceps muscle group and the primordial core. The primordial core, one of the five cognitive layers that were introduced in Chapter 5, comprises the control centers of all homeostatic actions, digestive actions, and fixed action patterns. (A reflex is a type of fixed action pattern.) Because the soma of the motor neuron is both the recipient of the inbound effector and the initiator of the outbound effector, it functions as a center of control for the patellar reflex;

therefore, it's part of the primordial core and can serve as its representative. Similarly, the spindle and the end plates jointly can serve as a representative of the quadriceps muscle group.

That the neural artifacts that conduct external social interactions, and those that execute internal bodily interactions, have similar architectures probably isn't a coincidence; on the contrary, it's likely that the former evolved from the latter; so, henceforth, the serial activation of a linked pair of innate effectors, the first of which is inbound and the second, outbound, will be called an internal transaction. All reflexes are internal transactions. So are all digestive and homeostatic actions.

ς

Within the brain of one participant, a social transaction can be conducted by as little as four neurons (not counting the neurons that constitute the object pyramids that represent the protagonists, or those that implement sensory input or muscular output.) And an internal transaction, such as the patellar reflex, can be executed by as little as two neurons. [51] It's largely due to such compactness that the brain is able to maintain a world model so populous that its owner believes that it's inhabiting a continuous, unambiguous objective reality. [52]

Despite the usefulness of this delusion, the fact remains that a world model is made up of artifacts that uniquely belong to the brain's owner; hence, one animal's model necessarily is different than another's. Consequently, whenever many have to act as one, although their motivations may seem identical, often they're not.

ς

During the 1960s, Paul MacLean proposed that the cranial brain of a vertebrate is a sequence of four structures (three nested neural shells, supported by a neural chassis.) Then, in the 1990s, Antonio Damasio proposed that the self is a sequence of four structures, each of which gives rise to a corresponding level of consciousness. To me, the similarity of their ideas seemed too great to be a mere coincidence.

Chapter 7: The Five Cognitive Layers of the Vertebrate Brain

The brain of a vertebrate is a biological machine that transforms sensation into motion [53] under the guidance of a subjective internal model of the world. This model, despite being unique to each animal, is sufficiently similar to those of the animal's conspecifics to enable communication and social transactions.

Like any other component of the body, the brain has been shaped over millions of years by evolution and natural selection. Because these processes are incremental and accretive, [54] the overall architecture of the vertebrate brain has come to consist of a sequence of five nested neural layers. (That the vertebrate brain comprises a sequence of nested layers is expounded by Paul MacLean in his book, "The Triune Brain in Evolution.") Each enclosing layer, together with those that it encloses, forms a fully functional brain, albeit a primitive one when compared to the brain that's formed by the next enclosing layer.

The innermost layer isn't located in the skull; it's embedded in a tube, which runs along the central axis of the body, whose job is to ingest and digest food and expel waste and toxins. This layer, which is the most essential and the most ancient, is called the enteric nervous system. By virtue of nerves and the bloodstream, the enteric nervous system is partially controlled by the cranial brain.

The cranial brain is divided into four cognitive layers. That there are four such strata [55] is a consequence of the fact that the architecture of the vertebrate brain was determined by four watersheds of evolution: moving in a purposeful way; constructing an explicit self; living as a lifelong member of an extended family; and objectifying complex sensory images. Each marked the emergence of a new suite of behaviors that were implemented by a new set of neural circuits.

Moving in a purposeful way is supervised by the primordial core, a cognitive layer that regulates homeostasis, smooth bodily motion, and fixed action patterns. (In the interest of brevity, we'll ignore smooth bodily motion, which is overseen by the cerebellum and the basal ganglia.) [56]

By subsuming the enteric nervous system, the primordial core also regulates digestion.

The primordial core conducts these activities by examining sensations, modifying them if necessary, and directing them according to the current needs of the body. (Internal sensations are called visceral input; external sensations are called sensory input.)

The primordial core is the lowermost and busiest of the four cranial layers. It's unique in that it's the only layer that connects to the brain's inputs and outputs. Consequently, of all the layers, the primordial core has the earliest, and the latest, opportunity to influence a decision. Furthermore, because of its access to the brain's inputs, the primordial core is uniquely aware of the states of all bodily components; the primordial core consolidates this information and passes it upward to the next cognitive layer.

For decisions that are conducted exclusively by the primordial core, in the interest of speed, the number of output options is limited. Consequently, the primordial core has a predilection for making decisions that are based upon dichotomies; within its limited judgment, a referent is either small or large, light or dark, or good or bad.

The primordial core physiologically encapsulates the spinal cord and the enteric nervous system, and thereby forms a complete brain.

Constructing an explicit self is supervised by the self shell. The state of the body that's passed to the self shell by the primordial core endows it with a rudimentary sense of self around which it assembles a personal identity. This enables it to act, in concert with the self object, as a proxy for the brain's owner within the owner's thinking. [57] By this means, the self shell conducts deliberate activities that benefit only the owner.

The self shell is the lowest layer that feels an imperative to stay alive. It responds to this drive by examining the inbound flow of every decision odyssey that passes through it, and directing it according to the parochial needs of the self object.

The self shell encapsulates the primordial core, and together they form a complete brain.

Living as a lifelong member of an extended family is supervised by the family shell. The family shell's main function is to act as an internal proxy for the family in order to influence the owner's thinking. It accomplishes this by examining the inbound flow of every decision odyssey that passes through it and directing it according to the parochial needs of the family. In so doing, the family shell modulates the self shell's thinking. The family shell can conduct this oversight even if the owner of the brain is alone and far away from the familial homestead. What's commonly called the conscience is a subset of this restraining influence, which is implemented via internal discussions between the self object and avatars that represent other members of the family. [58-59]

The family shell encapsulates the self shell, and together they form a complete brain.

Objectifying complex sensory images is supervised by the imaging shell. The neural artifacts that it produces usually are faithful facsimiles of their referents; but the imaging shell is endowed with a fertile imagination that regularly produces artifacts that are theoretical, mythological, vague, or downright false; [60] strange though it may seem, such non-faithful constructions are essential to social living, intelligence, language, and rational thinking.

That having been said, even the most ethereal products of the imaging shell are grounded in the body of the brain's owner; moreover, the inbound flow of data upon which they're constructed bears evidence of its passage through each of the lower layers. [61]

The imaging shell encapsulates the family shell, and together they form a complete brain, which is known simply as the brain.

§

At first glance, the primordial core's penchant for modifying sensations would seem to be deleterious to survival. [62] After all, wouldn't it be better for the brain to see things as they truly are?

Not always; in fact, many operations of the brain wouldn't work properly if they relied on a faithful representation of reality. For instance, in order to visually follow a moving referent, a mammal's brain passes information from the retina to the superior colliculus, a bump on the rear of the midbrain, which utilizes this data to coordinate muscles that control the movement of the eyes. But the information that's received by the superior colliculus isn't the same information that was received by the retina; by the time the retinal input has arrived at the colliculus, it's been transformed into spatial coordinates.

§

A decision odyssey enters the brain via sensory or visceral input, and exits via muscular or visceral output, figuratively tracing an arc upward, across, and downward through the brain. Consequently, each layer that it traverses gets an opportunity to influence the odyssey twice; once on the way up, and once on the way down. This ensures that the brain's owner gets the benefits of all of the layers, while avoiding the excesses of each.

§

Over the course of vertebrate evolution, whenever a circuit was added to a cognitive layer (after the layer's initial formation,) it had to be snaked through the neural mass that already existed therein. Circuits that are crammed together can develop cross-connections. If a new circuit came into close proximity with an older circuit, the former may inadvertently have connected to the latter.

This means that a decision odyssey that's propagating along the new circuit can inadvertently jump over onto the old circuit. If it thereby is deprived of cognition that's essential to its purpose, it may arrive at the primordial core, just before streaming out to the muscles and the viscera, without preparations that this omitted cognition would have provided. If the older circuit is of ancient evolutionary vintage, the brain's owner may revert to a primitive mode of behavior.

§

Computers today generate pictures in four different ways. Because these methods were invented at different times, during which computer technology was continually advancing, the storage-efficiency of each technique is superior to that of its predecessor. This is reminiscent of the process of visual objectification that was proposed in Chapter 1.

If, indeed, computer graphics is similar to visual objectification, then an exploration of the former is likely to improve our understanding of the latter.

Chapter 8: Computer Graphics and Vertebrate Vision

Most vertebrates understand the world through visual imagery. [63] This means that their brains must be inhabited by representations of external referents that are assembled from data that's derived from the retina. The human brain can house more than 50,000 such artifacts, [64] and can, on demand, conjure up the image of any one of them instantaneously. How does it accomplish this?

In order to answer this question, we must investigate how the brain objectifies a referent; and for this purpose, computer graphics can be used as an analog.

Within computer graphics, the term "pixel" denotes a tiny screen region that emits light of one particular color at a particular level of brightness. Pixels are grouped together in display groups of three: one for each of the primary colors, red, green, and blue; so, this system is called RGB. By judiciously setting the brightness levels of the pixels in each group, a computer can produce a full color image.

In addition to RGB, there's a color emulation technique called grayscale within which only black, white, and a finite set of specific shades of gray are displayed. On the screen, a gray shade can be produced by setting a display group's red, green, and blue pixels to the same level of brightness.

RGB and grayscale graphics in a computer are similar to color and nighttime vision in a vertebrate; [65] therefore, the term, "pixel," also is used to denote a photoreceptive neuron within the retina.

A neural structure that, when activated, reconstructs a visual image is a type of dispositional representation. A dispositional representation is an embodied executable program. Unlike a computer program, which is copied from memory and executed elsewhere, a dispositional representation is

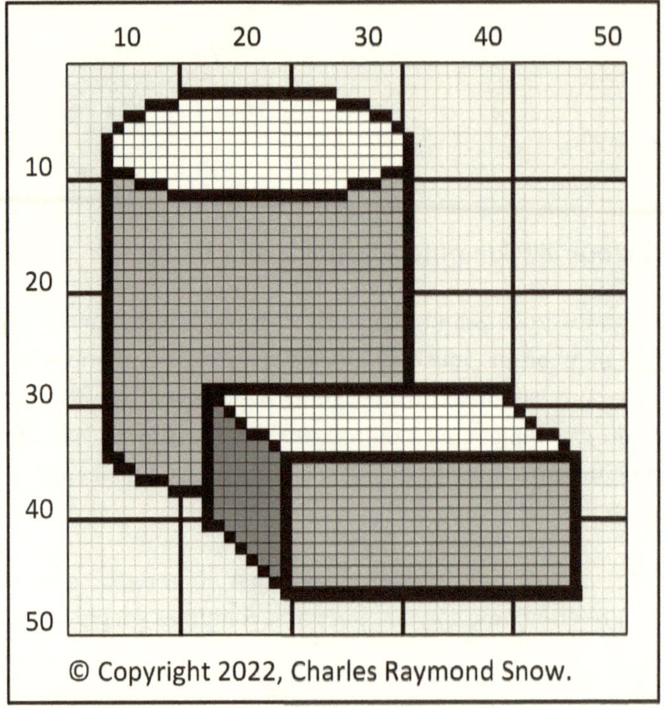

Figure 3: A Pixel Drawing
In the main window of a pixel drawing program, within
a 50-by-50-cell workspace, a picture of a cylinder and
a rectangular box might look like this.

executed in place. The brain has thousands of dispositional representations that reconstruct visual images; but we don't completely understand how they operate.

In contrast, a computer reconstructs a graphical image by reading in pixel values, or executing a set of instructions, that are stored in a file; if the file is readable, it's possible to determine how the data that it contains is transformed into an image.

Figure 3 shows a pixel image of a cylinder and a rectangular box. It was created on a desktop computer by utilizing an inexpensive commercial pixel drawing program. (Because a 50-by-50-pixel image is very small, in order to show you how it depicts the cylinder and the box, I had to magnify it; that's why the edges of the figures look jagged.)

248	248	248	248	248	248	248	248	248	248	248	248
248	248	248	248	248	248	248	248	248	248	248	248
248	248	248	248	248	248	248	248	248	248	000	000
248	248	248	248	248	248	248	000	000	000	255	255
248	248	248	248	248	000	000	255	255	255	255	255
248	248	248	248	000	255	255	255	255	255	255	255
248	248	248	000	255	255	255	255	255	255	255	255
248	248	248	000	255	255	255	255	255	255	255	255
248	248	248	000	255	255	255	255	255	255	255	255
248	248	248	000	000	000	255	255	255	255	255	255
248	248	248	000	236	236	000	000	000	255	255	255

Figure 4: A Numeric Representation of a Pixel Image

This table shows the numeric color codes of the first 12
cells, in the first 11 rows, of the image that's depicted
in Figure 3.

The program produces rectangular grayscale images that are made up of
square cells. Each cell represents one display group in which all three pixels
have been set to the same level of brightness.

In order to help the user, the program provides on the computer screen a
rectangular grid that functions as a workspace within which the user can
color individual cells. In Figure 3, the grid comprises 50 rows, each of which
contains 50 cells.

In a computer file, the drawing is stored as an ordered list of numbers, each
of which specifies the color of one cell. Each number represents a specific
grayscale color; 0 for black, 224 for dark gray, 236 for medium gray, 248 for
light gray, and 255 for white.

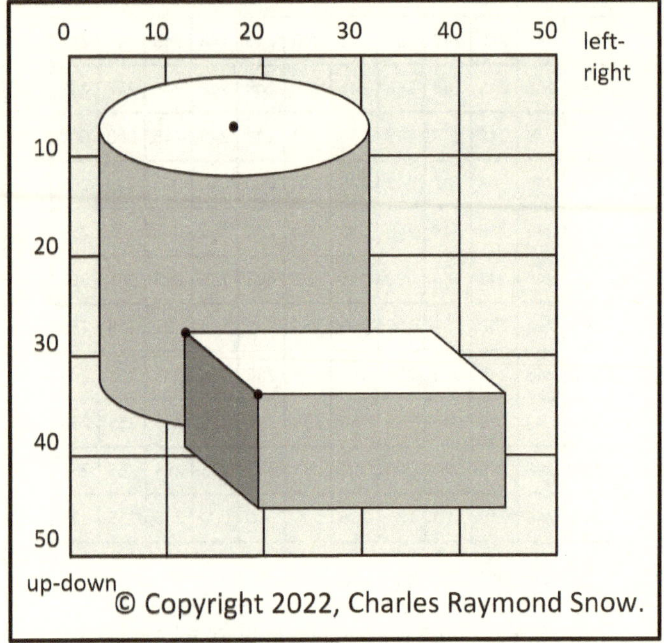

Figure 5: A Two–Dimensional Vector Drawing

In the main window of a two–dimensional vector drawing program, within a 50–by–50–unit workspace, a picture of a cylinder and a rectangular box might look like this. (The black dots are anchor points.)

Figure 4 shows a portion of the contents of this list. (The picture description header, which specifies the number of cells per row, isn't shown.) The list is a numeric representation of the image.

Whenever the graphics program is directed to re-display the image, it reads in the list from the file and assigns the first numeric value to the first cell within row 1; this causes the cell, which is located in the top left corner of the grid, to be colored in the appropriate shade of gray. (The shade that corresponds to the first numeric value.) Similarly, the program assigns the second numeric value to the second cell within row 1, which is located directly to the right of the first cell.

When it has finished specifying the colors of the first 50 cells, it assigns the next numeric value to the first cell within row 2, which is located directly below the first cell of row 1.

Polygon	Type	Anchor Left-Right Coord.	Anchor Up-Down Coord.	Width or Top Edge	Height or Left Edge	Color	Angle
rectangle	2	2	8	28	26	236	0
ellipse	1	18	32	28	11	236	0
ellipse	1	18	8	28	11	255	0
rectangle	2	19	34	25	12	236	0
parallelogram	3	12	28	25	8	255	30
parallelogram	3	12	28	8	8	224	60

Table 1: A Table of Two-Dimensional
Vector Drawing Instructions

These instructions, when executed in the indicated
order by a two-dimensional vector drawing program,
could produce the image that's illustrated in Figure 5.

Continuing in this fashion, the program builds up the picture, one cell at a time, until the image is complete. Because the numbers in the list all have values that are between 0 and 255, each can be stored within one byte, and, consequently, in the file, the drawing (that is to say, the data that's utilized to re-create it) occupies 2,500 bytes.

In practice, the number of bytes that are needed can be dramatically reduced by using repetition counts. For example, the first 110 cells of Figure 3, which constitute all of rows 1 and 2 and part of row 3, by virtue of being colored light gray, can be represented in the file by the ordered pair of numbers, 110, 248. This reduces the amount of file space that's needed to store this portion of the picture from 110 bytes to 2 bytes. The graphics program can detect such repetition counts and use them accordingly. (In order to avoid making Figure 4 needlessly complex, I refrained from using repetition counts.)

Suppose that a movie needed to be produced in which the cylinder remained stationary but the box moved forward. This would necessitate using the program to draw several versions of the picture, with the box being depicted progressively farther away from the cylinder. If these pictures were to be printed, stacked in order, and flipped like playing cards, they would show such a movie. If the movie were to contain only three pictures, all of which were to be stored in one file, then, within the file, the movie would occupy 7,500 bytes.

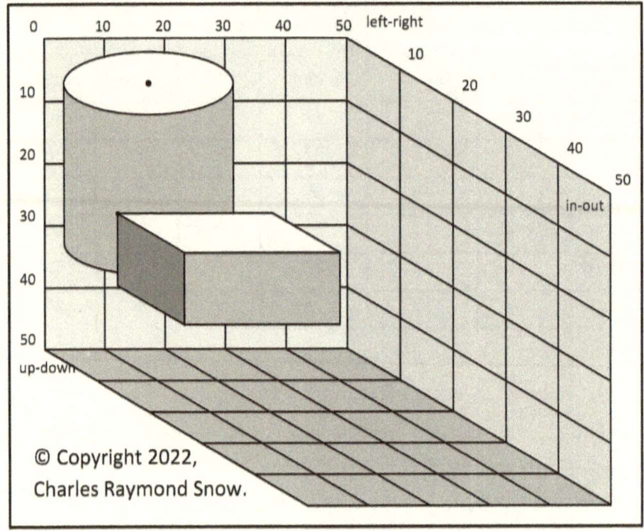

Figure 6: A Three-Dimensional Vector Drawing

In the main window of a three-dimensional vector drawing program, within a 50-by-50-by-50-unit virtual workspace, a picture of a cylinder and a rectangular box might look like this.

Figure 5 shows a two-dimensional (2D) vector drawing that's equivalent to the pixel drawing in Figure 3. A 2D-vector drawing is a drawing that's composed of polygons.

Unlike a pixel drawing, a 2D-vector drawing is stored in a file as an ordered list of instructions. Each instruction tells the computer to draw either a line or a polygon. In order to help the user, a 2D-vector drawing program provides, on the computer screen, a rectangular workspace within which the user can draw polygons; by judiciously sizing, coloring, and positioning them, the user can depict solid objects.

In order to create a 2D-vector drawing that's equivalent to the drawing in Figure 3, the cylinder and the box must be decomposed into pieces that can be represented as polygons. In Figure 5, the box has been broken down into one rectangle and two parallelograms, and the cylinder, into one rectangle and two ellipses. (Each ellipse is actually a polygon that has many sides.) The curving lateral surface of the cylinder has been simulated by merging the rectangle with the lower ellipse; this was accomplished by assigning the same color, medium gray, to both of them.

Solid	Type	Anchor Left-Right Coord.	Anchor Up-Down Coord.	Anchor In-Out Coord.	Width	Height	Depth	Color
cylinder	1	10	2	7	12	26	12	248
box	2	4	20	17	28	12	12	248

Table 2: A Table of Three-Dimensional
Vector Drawing Instructions
These instructions, when executed by a three-dimensional vector drawing program, could produce the image that's illustrated in Figure 6.

As the user of the program was drawing these shapes, the program would have composed a drawing instruction for each of them and then encoded each instruction as a sequence of numbers.

Such numbers are called parameters; they specify the type, location, dimensions, and color of the corresponding polygon.

A polygon's type can be denoted by a number; for example, in Table 1, an ellipse is denoted by the number one; a rectangle, by the number two; and a parallelogram, by the number three.

A polygon's location can be specified by the coordinates of a designated point that's situated somewhere on the polygon. Such a point is called an anchor. In Figure 5, the anchor point of each quadrilateral is its uppermost, leftmost corner. (The two parallelograms share the same anchor.) The anchor point of the upper ellipse, the one that represents the top of the cylinder, is its center.

In order to forestall the confusion that might result from seeing two anchor points within one surface, the anchor points of the rectangle and ellipse that constitute the side of the cylinder aren't shown; they are, however, specified in Table 1.

Table 1 contains a list of drawing instructions that might be utilized to generate the image in Figure 5. Each instruction is a representation of the corresponding polygon. Because all of the instructions' parameters have values that are between 0 and 255, one instruction occupies 7 bytes, and the entire drawing occupies 42 bytes.

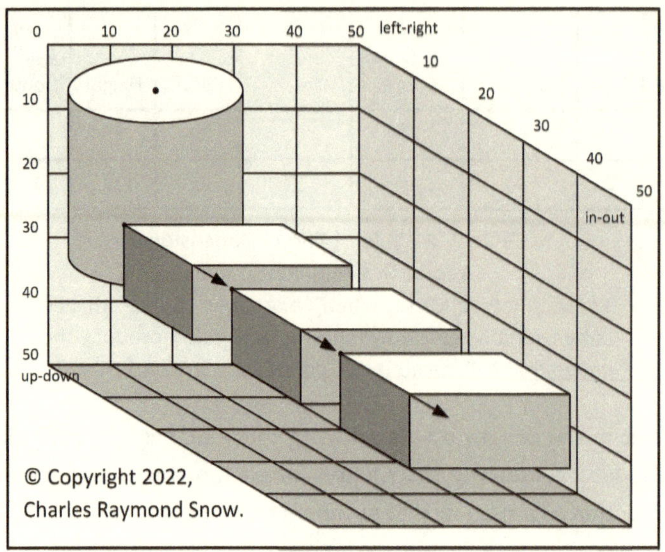

Figure 7: An Animation Vector Drawing

This Figure depicts a stationary cylinder and a moving rectangular box; it's a composite that shows the box, at three positions in its trajectory, as it might appear in the main window of an animation vector drawing program.

Whenever the graphics program is directed to re-display the image, it reads in the file containing the instructions and executes them in the specified order. (In the process of drawing the box, the program partially overwrites the drawing of the cylinder.)

The execution of each instruction produces an ordered sequence of directed lines, called vectors, each of which is specified by its two end points. Each point, in turn, is specified by two coordinates, the first of which is equivalent to a horizontal distance from the "up-down" axis, and the second, a vertical distance from the "left-right" axis. A closed figure is constructed by making the terminating end of each vector coincide with the originating end of the next, and by making the terminating end of the last vector coincide with the originating end of the first.

Solid	Type	Anchor Left-Right Coord.	Anchor Up-Down Coord.	Anchor In-Out Coord.	Width	Height	Depth	Color	Speed Left-Right	Speed Up-Down	Speed In-Out
cylinder	1	10	2	7	12	26	12	248	0	0	0
box	2	4	20	17	28	12	12	248	0	0	36

Table 3: A Table of Animation Vector
Drawing Instructions
These instructions, when executed by an animation
vector drawing program, could produce the images that
are suggested by Figure 7.

The program fills in the points between the end points of each vector, producing a figure that's made up of straight lines that, together, form the outline of the desired polygon. Then the area that's enclosed by the outline is assigned the specified color.

When all of the polygons have been constructed, the drawing is converted into a rectangular grid of grayscale cells; that is to say, the 2D-vector drawing is converted into a pixel drawing. Only then does the picture appear on the screen.

Having made a 2D-vector drawing of the cylinder and the box, the user could produce another three-flip-card movie in which the box appeared to move. This version of the movie, when stored in a file, would occupy only 126 bytes. Compared with the pixel version, this would constitute a 59-fold improvement in storage efficiency.

Figure 6 shows a three-dimensional (3D) vector drawing that's equivalent to the drawings in Figures 3 and 5. A 3D-vector drawing, like a 2D-vector drawing, is stored in a file as an ordered list of instructions. However, in a 3D-vector drawing, each instruction tells the computer to draw either a line, a polygon, or a solid that has polygonal sides. In order to help the user, such a program provides on the computer screen a virtual workspace within which the user can draw three-dimensional geometric figures.

Figure 6 comprises two such figures. The shade of gray that's applied to each facet is determined not only by the overall color of the corresponding figure, but also by the facet's illumination by an imaginary light source (which, for this picture, is conceived as lying somewhere above and to the right of the figures.)

Table 2 contains a list of drawing instructions that might be utilized to generate the image in Figure 6; because all of their parameters have values that are between 0 and 255, each instruction occupies 8 bytes, and the entire drawing occupies 16 bytes.

Having made a 3D-vector drawing of the cylinder and the box, the user could create yet another three-flip-card movie. In the corresponding file, this movie would occupy only 48 bytes. Compared with the pixel version, this would constitute a 156-fold improvement in storage efficiency.

Figure 7 shows an animation vector drawing in which the box is depicted at three moments during its progression. If the depictions at the second and third moments are ignored, then the drawing in Figure 7 is equivalent to those in Figures 3, 5, and 6.

An animation vector drawing, like a 2D or 3D vector drawing, is stored in a file as an ordered list of instructions, such as those in Table 3. If one of the figures is to be depicted as if it were in motion, then the corresponding drawing instruction must specify not only the object's type, position, dimensions, and color, but also its speed and direction of motion, which jointly are called its velocity. For instance, in the second instruction of Table 3, the box's velocity is specified as being 36 units per second in a direction parallel to the in-out axis. Its initial position is indicated by the coordinates of its anchor point, which are listed as being 4, 20, and 17, respectively; the coordinates of subsequent positions are calculated by the computer based upon the specified velocity.

In order to produce a movie that's equivalent to those that were described in preceding paragraphs, the user could direct the program to run the animation for a period of one second, and, during this time span, generate three snapshots, each of which is a three-dimensional drawing.

Because this version of the movie would be created by two instructions, each of which contained 11 parameters, its file representation would occupy only 22 bytes. Compared with the pixel version, this would constitute a 340-fold improvement in storage efficiency.

In order for the program to display this movie, it would run the animation, and thereby produce three 3D-vector drawings; then convert each 3D drawing into a 2D-vector drawing; and then convert each 2D drawing into a pixel drawing. These transformations are called, respectively, freezing, flattening, and rasterizing. Each of them has an inverse; a corresponding transformation that does the reverse. The inverse of rasterizing is called vectorizing, the inverse of flattening is called inflating, and the inverse of freezing is called animating. In general, vectorizing, inflating, and animating are much more difficult than freezing, flattening, and rasterizing; yet the vertebrate brain, seemingly without effort, routinely applies to pixel images the neural equivalents of vectorizing and inflating in order to objectify the referents that they depict.

§

Effective design is a matter of compromise, and the enormous benefit of converting a retinal image into the neural equivalent of a 3D-vector drawing comes at an enormous price: for by the time the vision system has completed the conversion, the original image has been wiped from the retina and been replaced by a new image that may have nothing to do with the preceding one. [66] Although this generally doesn't pose a survival threat, what is seen, in the internal world of the brain, isn't necessarily identical to what was there, in the external world of reality. [67] On those rare occasions in which the vision system makes a mistake, the brain may not detect it, for it no longer has access to the original data. [68] From that point forward, unbeknownst to the brain, its thoughts, simulations, and predictions may be flawed.

§

Having explored the similarities between computer graphics and vertebrate vision, let's revisit the objectification scheme that was proposed in Chapter 1 and see where it leads.

Chapter 9: Referent Recognition

Whenever a lion breaks cover and charges at an antelope, the antelope's fear response launches a large number of visceral and muscular actions that, together, cause the antelope to flee. Their rapid execution, one after another, is like the flow of a river. This virtual flow, which begins as sensation, passes through the body, and emerges as motion, is called a decision odyssey.

Within the antelope's brain, the decision odyssey that's been triggered by the sighting of the lion must, in some sense, touch a neural artifact that represents the lion; otherwise, the flow would be meaningless. Such an artifact is called an object.

We don't know precisely how the vertebrate brain constructs a visual object, but without an explanation, it's impossible to understand human behavior. So, in the interest of proceeding, in the following paragraphs, I'll elaborate the speculative explanation that I began in Chapter 1.

Because our aim is to understand social behavior, we're largely uninterested in an animal's interactions with non-animals. So, the neural artifacts that most concern us are objects that represent the animal, itself, members of its extended family, members of other conspecific families, friendly or contentious members of other species, and predators. Therefore, henceforth, for the most part, only such objects will be considered.

§

Visual objectification begins with a retinal image that represents a scene in the real external world. Neural signals that originate in the retina are passed through the thalamus to a region on the cerebral cortex. This region is known as the primary visual cortex, Brodmann area 17, the striate cortex, visual area 1, or area V1. (In general, we'll use the latter term.)

Area V1 is the first member of a sequence of cortical vision-related areas. How these areas break down, analyze, and reassemble information from the retina is one of the most studied subjects in neuroscience. But despite more than a century of research, only portions of this process are understood.

However, Roger Tootell has demonstrated that in the brain of a macaque monkey, and by implication, in that of a human, area V1 contains a nearly verbatim pixel copy of the image on the retina. Because of the wrinkled morphology of the cerebrum, this copy is a distorted version of the retinal image; but we'll ignore this complication.

This strongly suggests that vertebrate vision is largely a process of refinement, in which the pixel image in area V1 is subjected to a sequence of operations; and that these operations transform the image into a set of diverse pieces of information that are useful to the brain. For the purpose of understanding behavior, the most significant of these pieces is the visual object.

In the interest of simplicity, we'll assume that the internalized scene from which a referent is objectified occupies a single sheet of contiguous neurons in area V1, and that each neuron embodies one pixel of the corresponding image.

By incrementally analyzing and refining this image, the brain assembles an object that represents the referent. It accomplishes this by propagating the image, in a stepwise fashion, upward through an object pyramid whose base is the sheet of neurons in area V1. During this journey, it gradually circumscribes, analyzes, and refines the portion of the image that represents the referent.

(Because object pyramids cannot be assembled on the fly, thousands are created during fetal development, ready to be utilized when needed. [69] All of them share as a common base the aforementioned sheet of neurons in area V1. This common base is designated as level 1.)

Each neuron in level 1 is connected to a designated set of neurons in level 2. Whenever the level-1 neurons fire their axons, they modify the physical and chemical properties of the dendritic synapses of some of their corresponding level-2 neurons. In toto, they thereby produce in level 2 an encoded version of the image in level 1. As the image continues to be propagated upward through the object pyramid, the neurons of each level similarly modify the neurons of the next.

Meanwhile, extraneous details are discarded so that, eventually, the image (that is to say, its synaptic representation) depicts only the referent. Simultaneously, structural features, such as edges and surfaces, are identified, and are utilized to transform the referent's image from pixel to three-dimensional form. [70] The 3D form, in turn, is incrementally reduced in size [71] until it constitutes a minimal facsimile.

§

As the image travels from the retina, through the thalamus, and through the visual regions of the cerebral cortex, many related activities take place, some of the most important of which are the following:

1.　Information is sent to the hypothalamus, so that it can trigger an appropriate emotion;

2.　To the amygdala, so that it can engender an appropriate feeling;

3.　And to the superior colliculus, so that it can shift the direction of the brain's owner's gaze in order to follow the referent (if the referent is moving.)

4.　If the referent emits an odor, the odor is objectified by the olfactory nervous system;

5.　If it produces a sound, the sound is objectified by the auditory nervous system; [72]

6.　If the owner and the referent are primates, the referent's face is objectified by the facial part of the visual nervous system;

7.　And if the owner is a languaged human who concomitantly comes to know the referent's name, the sound of the name is objectified by the lexical part of the auditory nervous system.

Subsequently, whenever the brain regenerates the visual image, it also reconstructs the corresponding object. Concomitantly, it regenerates the emotion and feeling that were invoked when the object was initially constructed, and (via the response neuron) regenerates the images of the ancillary objects.

It's likely that these, together with other associated images, jointly cause the brain's owner to see the referent momentarily. That is to say, in order for the owner to see the referent in their mind's eye, regenerating the visual image probably isn't sufficient; it also may be necessary to simultaneously regenerate ancillary sensations (including emotions and feelings) and other images that are associated with the referent. We'll assume that this is so.

ς

It's likely that whenever the brain wants to regenerate a referent's image, it first resurrects the pixel image of the external scene from which the referent was objectified. How does it accomplish this?

One way by which it might do so is to utilize a duplicate pyramid, intertwined with the original, whose axons are oriented downward toward the base. The original pyramid is called the ascending half, and the duplicate is called the descending half, of the combined structure. (In forthcoming Figures, only the ascending halves are shown.)

Each synapse in the ascending half is innately connected, via a dedicated interneuron, to a corresponding synapse in the descending half. This enables the creation of the object to determine which descending neurons will be activated in order to resurrect the scene.

After the objectification process has completed, whenever the request neuron of the object pyramid is activated, it launches a descending cascade of neural signals that incrementally reassembles an image of the corresponding scene and deposits it in the base of the pyramid. This sets off an ascending cascade that entirely reconstructs the object. Concomitantly, it regenerates ancillary sensations and images that, together with the visual image, cause the brain's owner to briefly see the referent.

ς

The request neuron can be activated directly or indirectly:

In direct activation, if a remote neuron is axonally connected to the request neuron, then whenever the former fires its axon, it activates the latter.

In indirect activation, if a decision odyssey happens to pass through a neuron of the pyramid, it launches a cascade of neural signals within the selfsame pyramid. If the neuron is in the descending half, the cascade performs a partial reconstruction of the scene that contained the referent; if it's in the ascending half, it performs a partial reconstruction of the corresponding object. In either case, the brain realizes that something's amiss; so, when the faulty cascade reaches the top of the pyramid, instead of activating the response neuron (in order to inform remote parts of the brain that the object's been reconstructed,) the brain activates the request neuron, which launches a bona fide downward cascade that, when it arrives at the base, regenerates the scene's full image.

The regeneration of the visual image sets off an upward cascade that entirely reconstructs the object. [73] This causes the brain to replay the emotion, feeling, scent, and sound (and, depending on the species, the face and name) that were associated with the original construction. Besides causing the brain's owner to see the referent, the reexperiencing of so many ancillary sensations also endows the visual image with context and meaning.

Notwithstanding the verisimilitude of these sensory images, if they aren't accompanied by kinesthetic sensations from muscles that move the head or shift the eyeballs, the owner knows that it isn't actually seeing the referent. (That is to say, the animal understands that, currently, the referent isn't actually in the immediate vicinity.)

ş

After a referent has been objectified, whenever a decision odyssey happens to pass through a neuron of the corresponding pyramid, it sets off a chain of events that eventually causes the animal to see the referent momentarily. Another way of putting this is to say that every neuron in the pyramid is the initial component of a unique dispositional representation that conjures up a picture of the referent. Because these representations jointly account for all of the neurons within the object pyramid, and because only they can conjure the picture, it might just as well be said that the entire pyramid constitutes the visual object. [74] In other words, the object that represents the referent is one and the same as the pyramid in which the object was constructed.

§

The objectification scheme that's been described in the preceding paragraphs implies that different visual objects aren't entirely distinct; because they're all rooted in a single sheet of neurons in area V1, they necessarily overlap. It's conceivable that this commonality underlies a mechanism by which the thought of one referent can spontaneously bring to mind the thought of another. [75]

§

How does the antelope recognize the lion when it's re-encountered? In order to answer this question, we need to understand the concept of an information digest.

The primate brain has a special area that's exclusively devoted to facial recognition. This suggests that whenever a primate objectifies another primate, it also objectifies its face. We'll assume that this is, indeed, the case; and we'll call the product of the second objectification a facial visual object.

Having a special area for faces makes good sense because, in primates, rapid accurate facial recognition is essential to their highly social lifestyle. The need for speed rules out comparing images pixel-by-pixel; yet, clearly, some kind of comparison is needed.

In order for the brain to perform an objectification, it isolates the referent's pixel image from the rest of the scene that contains it; it then reduces the number of neurons that are needed to represent the referent by transforming the pixel image into a minimal facsimile.

However, it's possible to reduce the number of neurons even further. The resulting representation doesn't need to be absolutely faithful to the original; it only needs to be faithful enough to allow recognition.

With regard to faces, we know that such a thing is possible because we can easily recognize a public figure from a caricatured cartoon of his or her face, even if the cartoon consists of only a few drawn lines. Very likely, the human brain achieves this by reducing a facial image to a minimal set of readily measured, universal features, such as the relative distance between the eyes. It subsequently recognizes an individual by comparing their features with those of people whom it's already objectified.

But the brain has no facility by which it can store two sets of numbers and then compare the matching values, one pair at a time. So, what, exactly, is it comparing?

In a computer, a long sequence of data can be condensed by a mathematical algorithm into a much shorter sequence that corresponds uniquely to the original, and which, thenceforth, can serve as its proxy. Such a sequence is called a digest.

It's conceivable that, as the referent's image propagates upward through the object pyramid, the brain, in a non-mathematical way, transforms the referent's minimal facsimile into a digest. The transformation assigns greater weight to the referent's invariant attributes (such as the relative distance between its eyes) and lesser weight to its variable attributes (such as its apparent size.) The transformation produces, in the identification neuron, a sequence of voltages, the pattern of which embodies the digest.

How many voltages are needed, and how should they be modulated, in order to embody the digest? Assuming that the brain has the capacity to store 50,000 objects, 16 voltages, each of which persists for a duration that has two permissible values, one short and the other, long, might suffice. This encryption scheme is known as Morse Code. In Morse Code, the two durations are called "dot" and "dash," respectively.

§

In the present case, when the antelope first encounters the lion, its brain selects an unused pyramid and utilizes it to objectify the latter. Concomitantly, it produces, in the pyramid's identification neuron, a sequence of voltages the pattern of which embodies a digest of the lion's image. The identification neuron forwards the sequence to a neural structure called the visual recognition polygon that determines if the lion previously has been objectified.

If it hasn't, the selected pyramid is removed from the pool of unused pyramids, and the connection between its identification neuron and the recognition polygon is disabled. Thenceforth, the pyramid will uniquely be associated with the lion.

Subsequently, whenever the antelope re-encounters the lion, its brain reflexively assumes that it's seeing an animal that it's never seen before. So, it dutifully selects an unused pyramid, propagates the current image upward, and incrementally analyzes and compresses it. (We'll refer to the putatively-never-before-seen referent as the unknown animal and to the original referent as the known animal.)

During this process, a sequence of voltages that embodies the unknown animal's digest is produced in the identification neuron of the current pyramid.

Now the antelope's brain has the wherewithal to recognize the animal that it's currently confronting. In order to do so, it must compare the voltage sequence that represents the unknown animal with the one that represents the known animal. This comparison can only be made if the object pyramid of the former is connected to that of the latter. But such a connection cannot be created on the fly; it must be in place beforehand. Therefore, it must be innate.

Moreover, because during fetal development, it's impossible to predict which object pyramids will need to be connected together, it's likely that each is passively connected to all of the others, such that subsequent neural processes can selectively actuate the connections.

This means that if the antelope's brain has the capacity to store 50,000 objects, it must possess a neural structure that's topographically equivalent to a 50,000-sided polygon in which all diagonals (a little more than 1.2 billion of them) have been drawn. Most of them will never be used; such diagonals eventually are absorbed by the brain so that their resources can be recycled.

This structure is called the visual recognition polygon. It's illustrated in Figure 8, where, in the interest of simplicity, it's depicted as a pentagon. Each vertex of the pentagon acts as a proxy for a corresponding object pyramid, which conventionally is pictured below the appropriate vertex. (In Figure 8, only two are depicted.)

When the identification neuron of the current pyramid fires its axon, it transfers the voltage sequence that embodies its digest to the corresponding vertex in the recognition polygon, which distributes it to each of the other vertices; each of these, in turn, forwards the sequence to the recognition neuron of the corresponding visual object pyramid.

The goal of this widespread distribution is to determine if the voltage sequence of the unknown animal matches that of an animal that's already been objectified; that is to say, to determine if the sequence of the unknown animal is sufficiently similar to that of some other animal for them to be regarded as being identical. (That the sequences don't entirely need to match enables the brain to recognize an animal whose visible appearance has changed slightly, due to aging, for example.)

In order to make this determination, the brain must reconstruct all extant objects in order to regenerate their digests. But this will cause the corresponding images to be seen by the brain's owner. Such a torrent of visual images would overwhelm and possibly immobilize the owner. How can this problem be forestalled?

One way to do so is to suppress the regeneration of ancillary images and sensations. This can be achieved via an inhibitory neuron. For example, inhibiting the response neuron prevents the reconstruction and expression of olfactory, auditory, facial, and lexical images that may be associated with the referent. Without such ancillary images, the brain's owner cannot see the referent.

Whenever a recognition neuron is activated, it activates the corresponding inhibitory neuron, and then activates the corresponding request neuron. The request neuron, in turn, sets off a cascade that reconstructs the object without causing the brain's owner to see the referent.

In the present case, one of the many recognition neurons that are activated by the polygon belongs to the pyramid that originally objectified the known animal. The activation of this neuron sets off a cascade that reconstructs the corresponding object and, concomitantly, regenerates the voltage sequence that represents the known animal and loads it into the identification neuron.

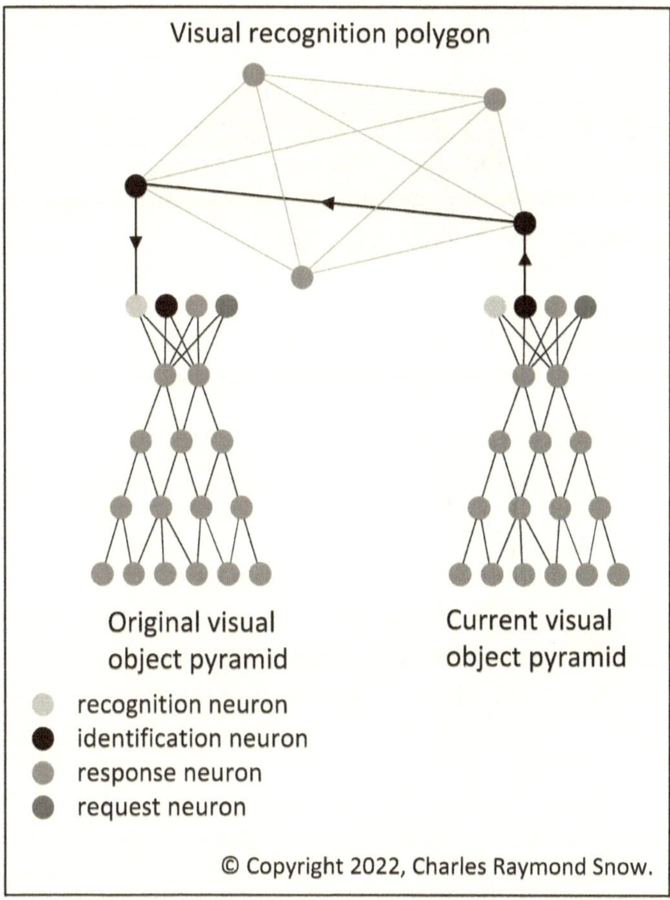

Figure 8: Recognition of a Referent

If the digest of one referent is sufficiently similar to that of another, the brain deems the referents to be identical.

The original pyramid now has access to voltage sequences that represent the known and unknown animals.

In order for the antelope to recognize the unknown animal, its brain must determine if the two sequences are sufficiently identical. One way by which it could do so would be to invert the sequence that represents the unknown animal, superimpose it upon the sequence that represents the known animal, and determine if the result is approximately null. (In other words, determine if the sequences almost, or completely, cancel each other.) We'll assume that the brain does, indeed, follow this procedure.

But in order for the two voltage sequences to be susceptible to being superimposed, they must arrive at the identification neuron simultaneously. One way to accomplish this would be for the recognition polygon to send its sequence repeatedly; by virtue of this tactic, eventually, the inverted sequence (which represents the unknown animal) would arrive at the identification neuron at the same time as the un-inverted sequence (which represents the known animal.) We'll assume that this is, in fact, what happens.

In the present case, when the identification neuron (of the known animal's pyramid) receives the two voltage sequences, the brain reacts by performing the following tasks:

- It superimposes the sequences, and determines that the result is null.

- It deactivates the inhibitory neuron.

- It activates the request neuron, and thereby reconstructs the known animal's object and regenerates the corresponding ancillary sensations. (This causes the antelope to momentarily see the original image of the lion.)

- It instructs the amygdala to generate a feeling that's epitomized by the word, "Aha!" This causes the antelope to realize that the known and unknown animals are identical. That is to say, it causes the antelope to recognize the lion.

§

The activation of the amygdala is crucial to the success of this process. Consider, for example, the following story, which is presented in the book, "Phantoms in the Brain," by V.S. Ramachandran and Sandra Blakeslee:

Dr. Ramachandran was consulted by the family of a man who had suffered a severe head injury in a motor vehicle accident. Upon returning home from the hospital, he no longer recognized his mother and father and demanded to know why two imposters were impersonating them. However, subsequently, when he placed a telephone call to his home and heard their voices, he immediately recognized them.

Dr. Ramachandran determined that the accident had destroyed connections from the patient's visual system to its corresponding region in the amygdala, but had spared like connections from his auditory system. Consequently, he couldn't experience an "Aha!" when he relied exclusively upon his sense of sight, but he could when he relied exclusively upon his sense of hearing.

§

The objectification scheme that's been described in the preceding paragraphs works not only for the sense of sight, but also for other sense modalities. For example, whenever two people are introduced to each other, it's likely that each of their brains constructs a lexical auditory object that represents the sound of the other person's name. The object is constructed in a neural pyramid that's rooted in an auditory cortex that receives input from the cochlea. Subsequently, any decision odyssey that happens to pass through this pyramid sets off a cascade that reconstructs the corresponding auditory object. This causes the brain's owner momentarily to hear the name being spoken, even if the cochlea is engaged in hearing other sounds.

This objectification scheme also makes it possible for the brain to perform a systematic mental search. For example, suppose that someone momentarily has forgotten the name of an acquaintance; this indicates that, in their brain, the response neuron of the acquaintance's visual pyramid, which connects to the request neuron of the corresponding lexical pyramid, isn't firing its axon.

Under these circumstances, the brain's owner can undertake a quick search through every available memory that involves the other person. If one of these episodes was emotionally significant, its reenactment may cause the amygdala to trigger a flood of excitatory chemicals in the brain.

Then, when the reenactment reconstructs the visual object that represents the acquaintance, the response neuron of the corresponding visual pyramid may be sufficiently stimulated to cause it to fire its axon. If so, it will trigger, in the corresponding lexical pyramid, a cascade that ultimately will cause the brain's owner to hear the sound of the other person's name.

(A mechanism by which the brain can access every memory that involves a particular person is proposed in Chapter 16. There are other methods by which an individual may trigger the recollection of a name; but in the interest of brevity, we won't investigate them.)

Taken together, the foregoing paragraphs suggest an explanation for the phenomenon of face-selective cells. (Such neurons also are known as "grandmother cells.") A face-selective cell is a single neuron in a patient's brain that, when artificially stimulated by an electrical impulse, causes the patient to see the face of someone with whom they're acquainted. The patient's brain may be found to contain several such neurons for the same individual. [76] Very likely, all of them lie within the neural pyramid that originally objectified the face of the acquaintance; the stimulation of any one of them triggers the execution of a unique dispositional representation that regenerates an image of this face.

§

When a human is angry with someone, he or she tends to interpret pessimistically everything that the other person says or does. Apparently, what we see isn't determined solely by our eyes; it's heavily influenced by the state of our bodies. In order to understand behavior, we need to know what states are possible and how they affect cognition and the senses.

Chapter 10: Violence, Sex, and Work

The fundamental imperatives of life are to eat, to avoid being eaten, and to make babies. [77] Each of them manifests itself in two ways: as a state of the body and as a suite of behaviors.

The state of a life-form's body is the physiological context within which it conducts a behavior. [78] In an animal, this context provides an emotional frame of reference that prepares its body for action. By limiting the number of frames to three, Nature simplifies decision-making and thereby enables animals to more quickly respond to threats and opportunities:

1. The violence context prepares an animal for fighting, fleeing, or freezing; it serves the highest imperative of life: surviving mortal dangers.

    However, the violence context isn't necessarily invoked if a threat is developing slowly; often, an animal in such a situation realizes the danger only when it's too late to evade it.

2. The sex context prepares an animal for bonding with others; it serves the second imperative: passing one's genes to the next generation. In social species that reproduce sexually, the sex context prepares males for competition over sexual access to females, females for selection of a suitable male, and both sexes for courting and copulation. The sex context also predisposes animals of both sexes, especially females, to protect and nurture their offspring.

3. The work context prepares an animal for obtaining the energy that powers the body; it serves the third imperative: obtaining food, water, warmth, and shelter sufficient to sustain life.

A bodily context serves as a physiological framework from within which an animal deploys accordant behaviors. These behaviors, like their corresponding contexts, are of three types:

1. A violence behavior is one in which an animal freezes, flees, or defends itself, or threatens, assaults, or kills another animal.

2. A sex behavior is one in which an animal solicits or engages in sexual intercourse. Bearing, raising, educating, and protecting children also are classed as sex behaviors; so are greeting and bonding activities that take place whenever groups or individuals meet, especially displays of affiliation such as touching, patting, hugging, or kissing.

3. A work behavior is one in which an animal obtains food via hunting, gathering, or scavenging. Eating, drinking, sleeping, seeking shelter, warmth, and dryness, managing bodily waste, nest-building, and tool-making also are classed as work behaviors. [79]

Distinguishing behavior from bodily context, while applying the same nomenclature to both, allows subtleties of animal activities, that otherwise might not be noticed, to be brought into focus. Consider, for example, that within a social setting, eating can be performed either angrily, seductively, or gluttonously. [80]

In all three cases, the same activity is being conducted; but because their contexts differ, the three situations are entirely different from each other.

Imagine that a male chimpanzee is eating a banana while glaring angrily at a rival male. In this instance, a work behavior is being conducted in the violence context. Why does this distinction matter? Because despite the tranquil appearance of this situation, it is, in reality, bristling with danger. Although the chimp is engaged in a work behavior, his brain and his body are undergoing a massive transformation whose aim is to prepare him for combat. This means that a vicious fight can erupt at any moment.

Primates are adept at reading the body language and facial expressions of other primates in order to interpret such ambiguous scenes and, if necessary, remove themselves to safety.

During the early phylogeny of animals, there was no distinction between context and behavior: violence behaviors were only performed in the violence context, sex behaviors in the sex context, and work behaviors in the work context. Even today, in simple animals, these restrictions apply. The capability of performing a behavior in a different context probably became useful only when animals began to live together in large extended families.

§

The distinction between behavior and bodily context is especially useful in elucidating play. Play activities usually are considered to be work behaviors, because they strengthen the muscles, teach important survival skills, and generally prepare an animal for obtaining the energy that's needed to sustain life. However, there are subtle differences between different kinds of play:

Whenever two toddlers are playing together, they're performing a work behavior within the work context. But when two immature males are roughhousing, chasing, or play-fighting, they're performing a violence behavior within the work context. Similarly, when a young female commandeers her infant brother in order to playact at mothering, she's performing a sex behavior within the work context.

However, when two mature males engage in an impromptu mock sparring session, they're performing a violence behavior within the sex context, because such play serves primarily to re-establish or reinforce their social bond.

§

So powerful is the influence of context over animal behavior that it frequently overwhelms the evidence of the senses. [81] (An example is presented in Figures 9 and 10.) The source of this compelling power is the emotional machinery that triggers the shifts between contexts. In vertebrates, these shifts are controlled by the hypothalamus.

The hypothalamus is one of the most anciently evolved structures in the brain and is formed early during fetal development. [82-83] In humans, it's located near the geometric center of the cranium and makes reciprocal connections with many parts of the brain.

Figure 9: A Female Crocodile Ferries a Turtle to the River

A crocodile who's recently hatched a brood picks up a turtle and ferries it to the river as she would if it were one of her hatchlings. Had the state of her body not been in the sex context, she probably would have eaten the turtle, instead.

The hypothalamus is the master controller of the body's homeostasis and a major contributor to the internal sense of self. Consequently, it's the most important organ in the primordial core of cognition and in the proto level of the self object. (The levels of the self object will be described in Chapter 11.) By virtue of its membership in the nervous system and its direct access to the bloodstream, [84] the hypothalamus is uniquely equipped to decide when the body's context must be changed.

The influence of the hypothalamus is enormous. For example, whenever the hypothalamus decides to swap an animal's somatic state into the violence context, it launches a cascade of fixed action patterns that changes many parts of the animal's body. [85] This transformation is known as the fear cascade or the fight-or-flight response. (Historically, it also was sometimes called the stress response; but due to the work of Hans Selye between 1940 and 1970, stress is now recognized as a phenomenon that's distinct from fear.)

The list of glands, nuclei, and organs that are affected by the fear cascade reads like a who's who of important bodily structures. In humans, it includes the pituitary, the amygdala, the hippocampus, the thyroid gland, the liver, the spleen, the adrenal glands, gastrointestinal blood vessels, the irises, the salivary glands, the skin, the hair, the heart, the lungs, the bladder, and the colon.

§

Because there are only three contexts, the body can be thought of as a finite state machine: a machine that, at any given moment, is in one of a limited number of pre-defined states. Because animals spend the majority of their lives in the work context, primarily in order to eat, the work context can be considered to be their default state.

But there's an exception: In a female vertebrate, the onset of the seasonal reproductive cycle (which for some mammalian species is called estrus) or the onset of pregnancy causes her body to swap into the sex context, which thenceforth constitutes her default state. If she consequently undergoes parturition, the sex context can persist for some time — as many as several months — during which she nurtures and protects her offspring. (In some species, it's the father who undergoes this change and assumes the role of nurturer and protector.) When her period of sexual receptivity ceases, or when her children no longer are completely dependent upon her, the default state of her body reverts to the work context.

The frequency of state changes depends upon the size and complexity of the animal's social group:

- Solitary animals change state occasionally; sex and violence are vital but relatively uncommon activities in their lives.

- Social animals change state often; living within an extended family requires frequent adjustments to changing social circumstances; sometimes these adjustments lead to fighting, but usually such combat isn't lethal.

- Highly social animals change state constantly. Primates, for instance, are inherently nervous animals. They never quite know, from one moment to the next, when something exciting or threatening is going to happen. To a large extent, their great intelligence is a side effect of their need to model internally a complex social world that's characterized by a constant train of delights and dangers.

§

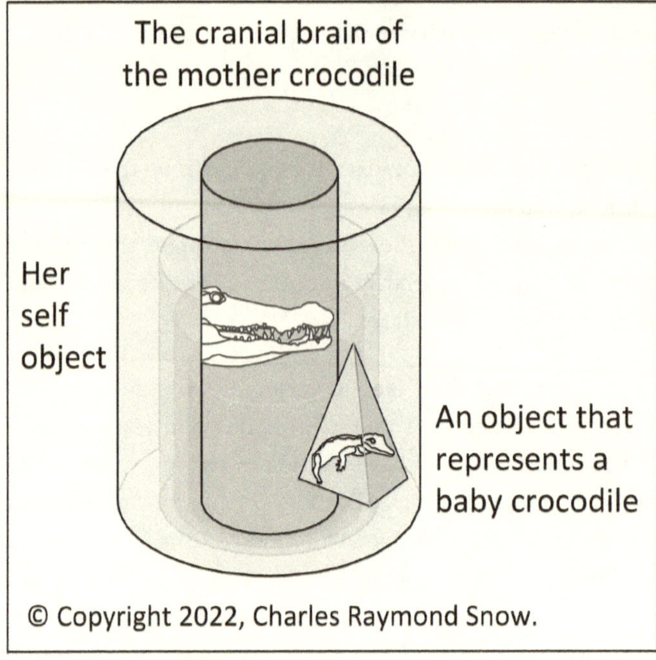

Figure 10: The Crocodile's World Model

Under the influence of the sex context, the mother crocodile who's depicted in Figure 9 mistakenly objectified the turtle as a baby crocodile.

Within the extended family group, as each animal cycles between the three bodily contexts, violent confrontations and sexual intrigues sometimes occur. In general, the family frowns on members who disturb the peace; everyone wants to enjoy, without interruption, the benefits of the work context, especially eating and resting.

But occasional fighting prepares males for real combat against invaders and sorts out their positions in the family's social hierarchy; and in hunter-gatherer societies, infidelities may serve to identify married couples who are poorly matched, so that they can be separated and remarried to partners with whom they're more compatible.

In other words, because it's occasionally useful, a low level of conflict is tolerated. [86]

§

	Initiator	Predicate	Recipient	Context	Behavior Type
1	David and Goliath	feeding on bananas		work	work
2	male baboon	charges at	David, Goliath	violence	violence
3	William	retreats from	baboon	violence	violence
4	David	retreats from	baboon	violence	violence
5	David	embraces	Goliath	violence	sex
6	David	threatens	baboon	violence	violence
7	baboon	threatens	David	violence	violence
8	David	embraces	Goliath	violence	sex
9	Goliath	threatens	baboon	violence	violence
10	David	threatens	baboon	violence	violence
11	baboon	retreats from	David, Goliath	violence	violence
12	baboon	slaps at	David	violence	violence
13	David and Goliath	retreat from	baboon	violence	violence
14	baboon	grabs bananas		violence	work
15	baboon	retreats		violence	violence

Table 4: A Table of Unitary Actions

This table contains a behavioral analysis of an encounter between the chimpanzees, David, Goliath, and William, and an aggressive male baboon, as it's described by Jane Goodall in her book, "In the Shadow of Man."

Violence, sex, and work, besides being behavior types and bodily contexts, are also powerful instinctive drives. If the satisfaction of such a drive is frustrated, an animal can become enraged.

Therefore, whenever two animals interact, each must be attentive to, and take into account, the emotional state of the other; if it doesn't, it's likely to blunder; and in the wild, a blundered social interaction can end badly.

§

The concepts of behavior type and bodily context are useful tools for understanding social interactions. In Table 4, for example, a squabble between four primates has been broken down into a sequence of actions and transactions. (Notice that within actions 5, 8, and 14, the context and behavior type don't match, but within all of the others, they do.)

How might such interactions be represented in the brain? And how can the brain remember the thousands of interactions that make up its owner's internal autobiography?

Consider the transaction in Table 4 that's made up of actions 6 and 7. Within the baboon's brain, action 6 can be modeled by a pair of neurons, the first of which represents David and the second, the baboon, itself. (In order to represent the protagonists, the neurons must previously have been connected to the corresponding object pyramids.) Action 7 can be simulated by a pair of neurons that represent the same protagonists, but in the opposite order. And, in both cases, the predicate "threatens" can be represented by an axon that originates in the first neuron and terminates in the second.

In order to forestall an infinite loop of signals, the neurons of the first pair must be distinct from those of the second. (This necessitates a connection between the two neurons that represent the baboon.) Therefore, excluding the neurons that make up the object pyramids of the protagonists, a memory of this transaction might require as little as four neurons.

This paucity of neural resources for storing one memory enables the brain to store many.

§

In order for a vertebrate to think about itself, its brain must contain an object that represents the selfsame animal. Such an object must be more complex than an object that represents an external referent; for besides representing the body, it also must undergo emotions, construct an autobiography, and feel an imperative to stay alive. But if there is such a thing, how does it work? And where, exactly, is it located?

Chapter 11: The Self

One of the fundamental activities of life is the construction of a self. Possession of a self greatly simplifies understanding the world, because it gives its owner the useful delusion of being at the center of space and time. This fiction affords a convenient point of reference from which the owner can estimate distances and time intervals. [87] Such estimates are essential not only to animals but to all forms of life. [88] This strongly suggests that, in the ancestral species of all extant living things, which lived approximately 3.5 billion years ago, [89] each individual also constructed a self, albeit a simple one. Such a being, if it could be observed today, would be indistinguishable from a bacterium; but how can a bacterium construct a self?

Before answering this question, I need to alert you to the fact that, from time to time, a prokaryote (a bacterium or an archaean) indiscriminately passes portions of its own genome to any other prokaryote that happens to be nearby, even if the latter is very different from the former. (This is one way whereby drug resistance can propagate from one type of prokaryote to another.) Consequently, the concept of biological species doesn't apply well to prokaryotes; but, in the interest of understanding the neural self, we'll proceed as if it does.

Only under exceptional circumstances is a bacterium ever alone; at all other times, it finds itself to be cheek by jowl with myriad other bacteria, not necessarily of its own species. In order to distinguish friend from foe, a bacterium employs two types of signaling molecules; one is secreted by all bacteria; the other, only by members of the species to which the bacterium belongs. Both diffuse through the medium in which the bacterium is living and dock with appropriate receptors on the cell membranes of other bacteria. Whenever this happens, the receptor changes shape and thereby conveys the signal to the cell's interior.

If a bacterium repeatedly receives simultaneous universal and species-specific signals, it presumes that it's among friends; if it receives universal, but no species-specific, signals, it presumes that it's in the presence of enemies; and if it receives no signals at all, it presumes that it's alone. (In this case, it may enter a dormant state, from which it subsequently can be awakened.)

All of this militates for a de facto self; for a bacterium, in effect, knows when it's alone, when it's in the company of enemies, and when it's in the company of friends; but neither the concept of aloneness, nor of enemy, nor of friend makes any sense without a countervailing concept of self. A bacterium holds this concept implicitly. Nevertheless, for all practical purposes, a bacterium's self functions just as effectively as a vertebrate's.

ξ

Vertebrates obsessively scan the environment for referents that can be internalized as objects. Usually, such artifacts are faithful representations of the things that they stand for, but sometimes, they're not. For example, despite the fact that it comprises an uncountable number of water droplets, a rainbow invariably is internalized as a single visual object. [90-91]

In a similar way, despite the fact that the self has many components, it invariably is perceived by its owner as a single entity. Because this entity seems to be insubstantial, it's conceived by most people to be a spirit that inhabits the body. This idea is convenient for day-to-day living; [92] but it's insufficiently concrete for science, and, more importantly, it can't be calibrated against evolution.

For this purpose, it's more useful to conceive that a vertebrate's brain contains an innate avatar that represents the animal, itself; [93] and that this avatar, which is called the self object, is an outgrowth of a widespread converging network that conveys to the brain a representation of the state of the whole organism.

Like any other component of the body, the brain has been shaped over millions of years by evolution and natural selection. Because these processes are incremental and accretive, the overall architecture of the vertebrate brain has come to consist of a sequence of five nested cognitive layers; [94]

and each enclosing layer, together with those that it encloses, forms a fully functional brain.

Because the self object is a subset of the brain and is involved in all forms of cognition, it intersects with all of the brain's layers. Consequently, the self object, too, consists of a sequence of five nested structures (to avoid confusion, we'll call them "levels" instead of "layers,") [95] and each enclosing level, together with those that it encloses, forms a fully functional self.

The first level of the vertebrate self object is called the enteric level. It's the lowermost, innermost, most essential, and most ancient of the five levels. The enteric level is identical to the enteric nervous system; that is to say, unlike the other four levels of the self object, the enteric level is one and the same as its corresponding cognitive layer. The enteric level supervises the digestive system and communicates, via nerves and the bloodstream, with the proto level.

The second level of the self object is called the proto level. (The terms, "proto," "core," "autobiographical," and "extended," are part of Antonio Damasio's nomenclature for the self.) The main components of the proto level are reflex control centers, which are located in the brainstem and the spinal cord, and homeostatic control centers, which are located in the cranial brain, along its central axis. [96-97] By functionally encapsulating the enteric level, the proto level also controls digestion.

The proto level receives signals, via the bloodstream and the nervous system, from all components of the body about their current states, [98] and merges them into a unitary feeling: a global feeling of the body. In order to construct the internal sense of self, as well as to maintain the higher strata of the self object, the proto level passes this feeling up to the next level.

Unlike higher levels of the self object, the proto level is a complete self in its own right, which, when referred to in this context, is called the proto-self. (Within classical Freudian psychology, the proto-self is known as the id.) This completeness bestows upon the proto level an independence that the other levels don't possess.

Because the proto level is a subset of the primordial core, it has a predilection for making decisions that are based upon dichotomies.

The third level of the self object is called the core level. By using, as a foundation, the feeling of the body that's being passed to it by the proto level, the core level assembles an individual identity for the owner of the brain. By virtue of this activity, the core level, unlike the proto level, feels a sense of self; consequently, it's the lowest level whose corresponding self is capable of experiencing the impulse for self-preservation.

The core level encapsulates the proto level, and, together, they form a complete self that we'll call the core self.

The fourth level of the self object is called the autobiographical level. [99] It's the lowest level whose corresponding self is capable of acting as a social being. Primarily from the animal's daily interactions with other members of its family, the autobiographical level assembles a subjective personal biography. The autobiographical level is able to achieve this because it possesses a sense of self, which it inherits from the core level, that enables it to function, within its owner's thinking, as a foil for each of the other members of its extended family.

The autobiographical level encapsulates the core level, and, together, they form a complete self that we'll call the autobiographical self.

The fifth level of the self object is called the extended level. [100] The extended level assembles an internal autobiographical narrative, which it recites continually to itself. By using the sense of self (that it inherits from the autobiographical level) as the nucleus around which to organize this never-ending story, the self that corresponds to the extended level is able to function competently both as an individual and as a member of the family to which the animal belongs. [101]

In humans, the extended level has a predilection for thinking in abstract terms, and, consequently, has a tendency to value symbolic concepts more highly than concrete facts. In the modern world, the extended level's penchant for ideal thinking enables a human who possesses the abstract notion of a nation to function competently as a citizen.

The extended level encapsulates the autobiographical level, and, together, they form a complete self that we'll call the extended self, or simply the self.

Because the self is coextensive with the self object, they are one and the same; that is to say, the self is identical to the self object.

§

The self object harbors a suite of assumptions that make it easier for an animal to make sense of the world. [102] For instance, the proto and core levels presume that they exist in a place known nonverbally as "here" and at a moment known as "now." [103] The autobiographical level presumes that it exists at the center of the family, in a role known as "me." It also presumes that its biography extends from some bygone time to the moment that it knows as "now"; a span of time that's known as "the past." The extended level, by virtue of its capacity for abstract thinking, can simulate events that haven't yet occurred; consequently, it presumes that its biography will extend from "now" into a span of time that's known as "the future." Although such pragmatic assumptions generally are helpful, they aren't necessarily features of reality.

§

An anthropoid (a gorilla, orangutan, bonobo, chimpanzee, or human) frequently talks to itself. Its brain conducts such conversations by directing its linguistic output to a neural artifact that's identical to the self object. Of course, the self object is so large that to fit a second instance of it within the brain is impossible. Instead, the brain utilizes a loop-back connection at the base of the primordial core to temporarily patch its linguistic output into its linguistic input (thereby bypassing the real external world); in other words, it assumes the role of a speaker in order to emit a message and then assumes the role of a listener in order to absorb it. Then, like a lone chess player who's rotated the chessboard in order to play against themselves, the brain formulates a response, and, once again, assumes the role of a speaker. It continues, in this manner, to loop output back into input, each time analogously rotating the chessboard, until the conversation ends.

Such internal verbal dialogs commonly are called "thinking." [104]

An anthropoid also regularly conducts internal conversations with avatars that represent other members of its extended family. Whenever such dialogs occur, the family leadership virtually reminds the self object of its obligation to follow the family's rules; this continual admonishment is the substrate upon which shame, virtue, guilt, and the conscience are built. [105]

Other vertebrates conduct such conversations nonverbally. For instance, if a dog does something that's been forbidden by its master (who previously has been accepted by the dog as the highest-ranking member of its family,) it feels shame, and, in many instances, when subsequently confronted by its master, involuntarily reveals its culpability.

§

All animals conduct internal nonverbal dialogs. [106] In vertebrates, such conversations are undertaken by all levels of the self object; but, by far, the proto level is the most talkative. The proto level conducts internal nonverbal dialogs with muscles, glands, organs, and neural structures, [107-108] and with itself. (Such conversations can be initiated either by the proto level or by the other party.)

For instance, the execution of the patellar reflex can be conceived as a short nonverbal dialog in which a quadriceps muscle talks to a reflex control center in the spinal cord, and the control center responds by talking to the quadriceps muscle. [109] Within such a dialog, the control center functions as a stand-in for the proto level of the self object, of which it is a part.

§

Over the course of evolutionary history, as animals competed against each other, their brains were subjected to natural selection. The brains that prevailed were those that most accurately represented the real external world. Consequently, the objects that the brain creates are, for the most part, incorruptible; they seek at all times, insofar as they're able, to remain true to objective reality.

The self object, however, isn't a facsimile of a referent that exists outside of the body; consequently, the self object, unlike other objects, isn't incorruptible. Its primary mission isn't to faithfully represent a referent, but rather to diligently manage the body. Its guiding star isn't external reality, but rather its own subjective internal feeling of the body. This feeling compels the self object to believe that anything that causes it to feel good is, itself, good, and that anything that causes it to feel bad is bad. Consequently, the personal identity that's synthesized by the self object is highly subjective and constitutes little more than a transiently useful myth. [110]

That the self object's conception of itself is a mythology, rather than the absolute truth, is a consequence of the limits of knowledge; for the only things that the self object can know are the contents of its owner's brain. This information necessarily is incomplete, inaccurate, and subjective. Why?

Because its aim isn't truth; it's survival. [111] To this end, the self object has been trained over millions of years of evolution to alter, or even ignore, sensory input in a self-serving manner. Consequently, its owner's worldview is inveterately subjective. In general, this subjectivity does no harm to the owner; but whenever the owner engages in a social transaction, its worldview is exposed to that of another. If the two parties harbor conflicting views of the external world or of each other, trouble usually follows. [112]

Chapter 12: Sensation and the Sense of Self

Whenever a mammalian baby is hungry, it cries and thereby gains the attention of a nearby caretaker, usually Mother, who immediately feeds it. The baby employs the same tactic whenever it's sick, frightened, too hot, too cold, or otherwise uncomfortable. This suggests that crying is enabled by a network that conveys sensations from all parts of the body to a single location in the brain, where they're consolidated into a unitary feeling. Then, some relatively simple neural process determines whether the feeling is good or bad, and, if bad, launches crying behavior.

As we now will see, the body-wide network that enables crying is the foundation of the self object, and the unitary feeling that it produces is the foundation of the internal sense of self.

§

All vertebrates possess at least one two-dimensional array of sensors, the retina, for instance, that forms exquisitely detailed images of the real, external world. [113] If an image that appears on this surface depicts a referent that the brain deems to be significant, the brain recruits a preexisting neural pyramid that's rooted in the array and utilizes it to transform the image into a neural object. This capability is a prerequisite for intelligence; indeed, intelligence may be more a consequence of superb objectification than of nimble reasoning. [114]

Because the brain thinks that the body proper resides in the real external world, it senses components of the body in a way that's similar to that by which it senses external referents. [115]

Nevertheless, the methods necessarily differ because, for an external referent, the brain is interested in its perceptible manifestations (such as its sound, smell, or visible appearance); but for a component of the body, the brain is interested in its physiological state.

Some bodily components convey their states to the brain by secreting molecular messengers into the bloodstream. [116-117] The proto level of the self object has portals to the circulatory system via which it can sample such messengers. If the messengers reveal that some homeostatic parameter isn't within its acceptable range, an appropriate control center within the proto level restores things to their proper state.

The remaining components of the body report their states to the brain via the nervous system. Accordingly, every muscle, bone, joint, gland, organ, and epithelial surface has an embedded array of neurons (which typically are noncontiguous) that conveys to the brain a sensory image of the state of that component.

Some components contain multiple kinds of arrays. The skin, for example, has separate arrays for sensing body position, pressure, pain, and temperature.

If the component is large, the embedded array is divided into sub-arrays, each of which innervates a specific part of the component. In the interest of simplicity, we'll use the word, "array," to denote either an array or a sub-array.

Each array is the base of a neural pyramid that conveys to the brain an image of the state of the corresponding component. As the image ascends the pyramid, it's transformed from a collection of sensory data into a sequence of voltages, which, via an apex neuron, is passed to the proto level of the self object. If the sequence indicates that the component is in distress, the proto level responds by launching remedial actions.

In contrast to external images, which typically are handled one at a time, all of the body's internal images are handled simultaneously; for, in order to maintain homeostasis, the brain needs to be aware at all times of the status of all bodily components. It's likely that, to this end, each internal sensory array continually launches a cascade, upward through its pyramid, that informs the brain of the current state of the corresponding component.

§

The concentration of so many apex neurons in the basement of the brain affords to it an opportunity to integrate their signals. One way to do this would be to make an axonal branch of each apex neuron serve as a basal element of yet another neural pyramid. We'll assume that this is, indeed, the case, and we'll call this structure the top-level pyramid. The summation of internal sensory data that's constructed by the top-level pyramid manifests itself to awareness and contemplation as a unified feeling of the body; [118] upon this foundation, the brain constructs the internal sense of self.

The top-level pyramid, together with the many and various internal sensory pyramids that it consolidates, form a gigantic neural pyramid whose base extends throughout the body. This body-wide network is effectively an additional level of the self object. Indeed, the proto level of the self object is an outgrowth of this network.

It's likely that the self object and the body-wide network jointly form a functional unit, which we'll call the self object pyramid. [119-120] Like other object pyramids, the self object pyramid has apex neurons via which it interacts with other neural structures. (These are distinct from the apex neurons of the pyramids that it consolidates.)

§

It's natural for an animal to be self-centered; so, from the viewpoint of the brain, there's simply no point in making any decision that doesn't involve the self; but to say that every decision involves the self is tantamount to saying that every decision odyssey passes through at least one of the neurons of the self object. It's conceivable that, by so doing, the odyssey sets off a cascade that transforms the unified feeling of the body into an explicit awareness of the self; in other words, it causes the animal who owns the brain to momentarily be consciously aware of itself.

Such an event, together with an "Aha!" generated by the amygdala, might enable an animal to recognize its own reflection in a mirror. (Some chimpanzees, bottlenose dolphins, and Asian elephants, and all humans who are more than 18 months of age, can do so.)

§

Every event that impinges upon the brain's owner perturbs some part of its body, triggers internal sensations, and ultimately alters the unified feeling of the body; moreover, because the body-wide network that constructs this feeling is the foundation of the self object, every event also modifies the self object. [121] But because no two individuals can experience precisely the same sequence of events, no two self objects can be identical; that is to say, every self object is unique.

ξ

By the beginning of the current millennium, 4,000 Americans per year were being diagnosed with dissociative identity disorder. Does the concept of the neural self allow for the existence of multiple persons within one body?

Chapter 13: Multiple Personalities

Between 1988 and 1999, counselor and motivational speaker John Bradshaw popularized the idea that everyone has a virtual inner child of whom he or she is generally unaware, and that the memories and impressions of this persona can be useful aids during psychotherapy.

Bradshaw's idea that an adult harbors an additional personality was foreshadowed by a putative psychiatric condition called dissociative identity disorder (which originally was known as multiple personality disorder.) Awareness of this affliction greatly increased after 1957, when a motion picture entitled "The Three Faces of Eve" was released. The film depicted a woman who possessed three distinct personalities, one of whom was unaware of the other two.

To date, no reputable scientific authority has accepted either dissociative identity disorder or the inner child as being a genuine neurological phenomenon. Topographic psychology asserts that the architecture of the self object precludes the existence of more than one adult personality within the same body; but it doesn't preclude the existence of an inner child.

§

Because the self object occupies such a large amount of neural real estate, a human can have only one. They can, however, have more than one self. In fact, they have four (the proto-self, the core self, the autobiographical self, and the extended self,) each of which is associated with a corresponding level of the self object.

If a given level were to be disabled (effectively disabling all of the levels above it as well) then the self corresponding to the level below would assume control of the body. However, if the autobiographical self was in charge, it would consider the interests of the brain's owner to be subordinate to those of the family; and if the proto-self was in charge, the brain's owner couldn't survive without constant supervision by someone else. Consequently, only the extended and core selves are capable of managing the body in the owner's best interests.

Suppose that the extended self wanted to talk to the core self. Naturally, it would use its verbal language, either aloud or silently. But the core self cannot speak because it doesn't have access to resources within the family and imaging shells that are essential to spoken language. So, it would have to respond to the extended self by utilizing the language of the body. For instance, if the extended self were to ask, "How're you doing?" the core self might reply by smiling.

If the extended self were to succeed in communicating with the core self, what would it discover about its new acquaintance?

Because the core self can't access the family shell, it doesn't know how to conduct social relations. Until now, it has known only itself and Mother. Excluding these two relationships, the core self has lived a cloistered life, inhabiting only one place, here, and only one moment, now. And because it doesn't speak in a verbal language, it's largely incapable of being deceptive.

In short, the extended self would discover a being who's uncomplicated and forthright, but who doesn't possess the power of speech; in other words, someone who's much like a preverbal child.

§

We now are ready to investigate such high-level behaviors as thinking, speaking, and storytelling. All three require an ability to conduct transactions.

Chapter 14: Transactions

A vertebrate's behavior largely is determined by its internal autobiography; [122] a private history that affords it a framework within which it can evaluate a current threat or opportunity. An internal autobiography is read and modified repeatedly by its author. [123-124] Each chapter consists of a series of binary social transactions that are conducted while the animal's bodily context is in a particular state. A binary social transaction consists of one animal performing a unitary action upon another, and the latter performing a reciprocal action upon the former.

A boxing match, for instance, is a series of binary social transactions within which one fighter strikes another, and the latter reacts by striking the former. [125] Within each boxer's brain, as the fight is progressing, each exchange of blows is transcribed into a neural record that constitutes a dispositional representation. The representation comprises two linked effectors: the inbound effector corresponds to an action that the other boxer has just performed upon the owner of the brain; and the outbound effector corresponds to an action that the latter is about to perform upon the former. The linkage consists in the fact that the recipient of the inbound effector is one and the same as the initiator of the outbound effector. This common artifact is a neural avatar called the self object.

It's likely that such a representation is constructed and stored just past the end of the boxer's internal autobiography, and thereby is appended to it. By this means, it serves not only as a mechanism by which he can react to his opponent in the present, but also as a mechanism by which he can recall the transaction in the future.

In this way, the entire fight is recorded as a coherent sequence of records. Such a sequence generally is called a memory. Recalling the memory consists of executing the records, one after another, while suppressing muscular output. (A way by which the brain might execute an autobiographical record is suggested in Chapter 16.) Their being serially connected makes it easy to replay the episode from start to finish, but difficult to play it backwards or to begin in the middle.

ş

Sometimes, either the inbound half of a transaction, or the outbound half, or both, consist of multiple unitary actions. For example, suppose that one boxer strikes another, puts him in a clinch, and pushes him against the ropes before the other man can react. Under these circumstances, the representation in the first man's brain of the outbound half of the transaction comprises three effectors, as does the representation in the second man's brain of the inbound half.

ş

Dispositional representations that conduct or reenact external social transactions reside in, and are executed by, the cranial brain; but there also are dispositional representations that conduct internal bodily transactions. Such representations reside in, and are executed within, the body proper and are mediated by either the brainstem, the spinal cord, or the enteric nervous system. In such a case, the internal representation of each component of the transaction is one and the same as the component, itself; and the protagonists of the transaction are organs, glands, nuclei, neural somas, neurons, or neuron-like structures such as muscle spindles or motor end plates. [126]

The patellar reflex is a good example. [127] The patellar reflex is an innate, automatic bodily transaction that's enabled by a congenital dispositional representation. The dispositional representation comprises two effectors. The initiator of the inbound effector is a muscle spindle that's located in one of the quadriceps muscles; the predicate is the dendritic-axonal projection of a pseudounipolar sensory neuron, which connects the spindle to a soma that's located in one of the lumbar vertebrae; and the recipient is the selfsame soma. The initiator of the outbound effector is the soma; the predicate is the axon of the corresponding motor neuron, which connects the soma to an ensemble of end plates that are located in the same muscle as the spindle; and the recipient is the ensemble of end plates. In both effectors, the action that the initiator performs is to send a neural signal to the recipient. Whenever the first effector is executed, the second is executed automatically.

Because the spindle and the end plates are components of the muscle to which they belong, and because the muscle, in turn, is a member of the muscle group to which it belongs, the spindle and the end plates jointly can serve as a representative of the quadriceps muscle group. Similarly, because the soma of the motor neuron is the control center of the reflex, and because all such control centers are components of the proto level of the self object, the soma can serve as a representative of the proto-level.

But the proto level is identical to the proto-self; therefore, the patellar reflex constitutes an innate embodied transaction between the quadriceps muscle group and the proto-self. Such an exchange is called an internal transaction.

All reflexes are internal transactions. So are all homeostatic and digestive actions.

§

Experienced fighters have observed that a boxing match is like a conversation in which the participants trade punches instead of words. [128] This similarity between fighting and conversing is more than a coincidence; on the contrary, like an exchange of blows between two boxers, an exchange of words between two interlocutors is a binary social transaction. [129] This suggests that speech evolved from nonverbal social transactions. Moreover, the architectural similarities between social and internal transactions suggest that the former evolved from the latter. All of this implies that the development of language, which would seem to have begun in the brain, ultimately began in the innate internal activities of the body.

Chapter 15: Analogizing, Sequencing, Tracking, and Thinking

In their book, "Surfaces and Essences," Douglas Hofstadter and Emanuel Sander suggest that analogies lie at the heart of all forms of thinking, and that the brain continually constructs analogies, many times per second. Let's examine this proposal and see where it leads.

Inference is the process of constructing a sequence of ideas in which each idea leads to the next. This kind of sequence variously is referred to as "a train of thought" or "a chain of reasoning." The machinery that produces an inference must be capable of assembling, within seconds, a long chain of ideas of disparate types. This suggests that, although an inference is made on the fly, the neural structure that represents it and within which it's constructed is in place beforehand; therefore, the structure must be innate.

An analogy is a simple form of inference. An explicit analogy is one that expresses a relationship between four elements in which the first is related to the second as the third is related to the fourth; if its elements can readily be objectified, then a neural representation of such an analogy can be based upon the corresponding objects. Very likely, the representation is a linked list of four neural artifacts (which are called pointers) in which the first three have mono-directional connections to their successors in the list, and all four have bidirectional connections to their corresponding object pyramids.

In order to form an explicit analogy, the four object pyramids (that is to say, the pointers that represent them) must be coupled together via neural connections, one to another. But such connections cannot be created on the fly; they must be in place beforehand. This means that they must be innate. Moreover, because during fetal development, it's impossible to predict which object pyramids will need to be connected together, it's likely that each is passively connected to all of the others, such that subsequent neural processes can selectively actuate the connections.

In particular, if the brain has the capacity to store 50,000 objects, it must possess a neural structure that's topographically equivalent to a 50,000-sided polygon in which all diagonals (about 1.2 billion of them) have been drawn. Very likely, the pointers that represent an explicit analogy are vertices of such a polygon.

In order for the brain to be capable of constructing analogies continually, it needs many such neural polygons. Because they all are topographically identical, in order to minimize the number of connections between them and the object pyramids that they reference, it's likely that they're stacked, one upon another, like so many platters.

§

In order for a brain to conceive an analogy, it doesn't necessarily have to possess a verbal language. All that it needs are neural artifacts that represent the relevant referents, and a mechanism by which it can selectively actuate connections that link them together.

This makes it possible for a non-human animal or a non-languaged human to create an analogy.

For example, suppose that a toddler (a boy) who as yet cannot speak conceives the nonverbal equivalent of, "I am to my father as my sister is to my mother." Very likely, this analogy is constructed and stored in a neural polygon stack, such as the one that's depicted in Figure 11.

In the present case, the boy, by making this analogy, has inferred that the relationship between his sister and his mother bears a strong resemblance to the relationship between him and his father; consequently, he now is in possession of a fact that he didn't possess before he constructed the analogy.

A mathematical proportion is an analogy; for to say, for example, that "2/3 = 4/6" is equivalent to saying that "2 is to 3 as 4 is to 6."

An analogy is a powerful aid to the boy's reasoning because whenever he makes one, he automatically gets seven additional analogies for free.

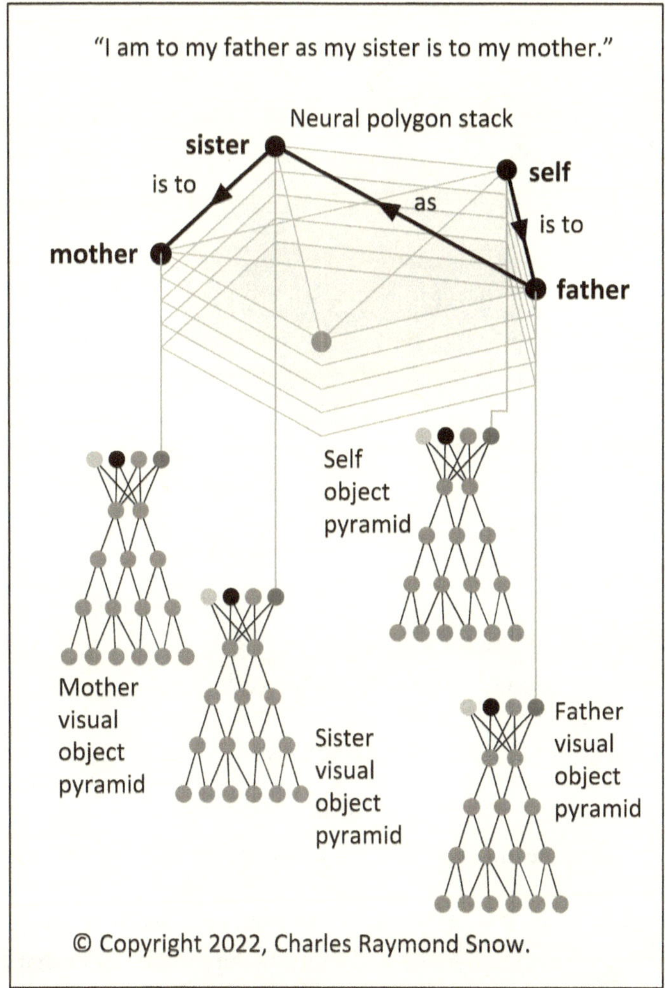

© Copyright 2022, Charles Raymond Snow.

Figure 11: The Neural Representation
of an Explicit Analogy

An explicit analogy can be represented by four vertices and
their mutual connections within a neural polygon stack.

For instance, the analogy, "I am to my father as my sister is to my mother," when the subject and object of each clause are swapped, yields another analogy, "My father is to me as my mother is to my sister."

Similarly, the proportion, "2/3 = 4/6," when the numerator and denominator of each fraction are swapped, yields another proportion, "3/2 = 6/4."

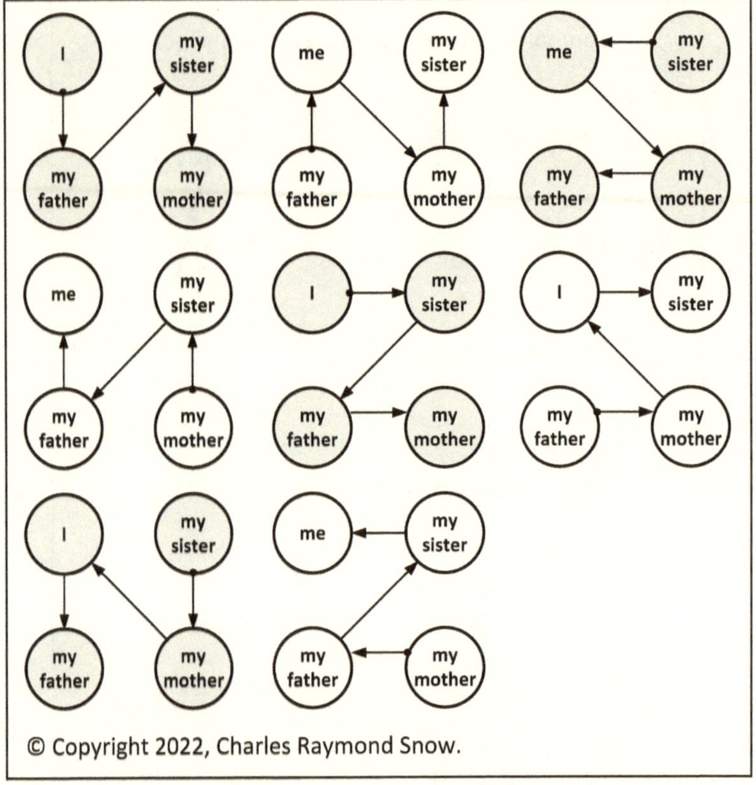

Figure 12: A Family of Analogies

One valid analogy gives rise to seven others.

More generally, once a valid analogy has been encoded in a polygon stack, any other zigzag path (when viewed from the top of the stack) that connects pointers to the four objects in question and that doesn't cross itself, encodes an additional valid analogy.

By way of counterexample, "2/6 = 4/3" doesn't constitute a valid proportion because, as is shown in Figure 13, the first and third connections of its neural representation cross each other.

ç

In the present case, during the process of creating his analogy, the boy must have visualized sequentially, within a brief period of time, himself, his father, his sister, and his mother.

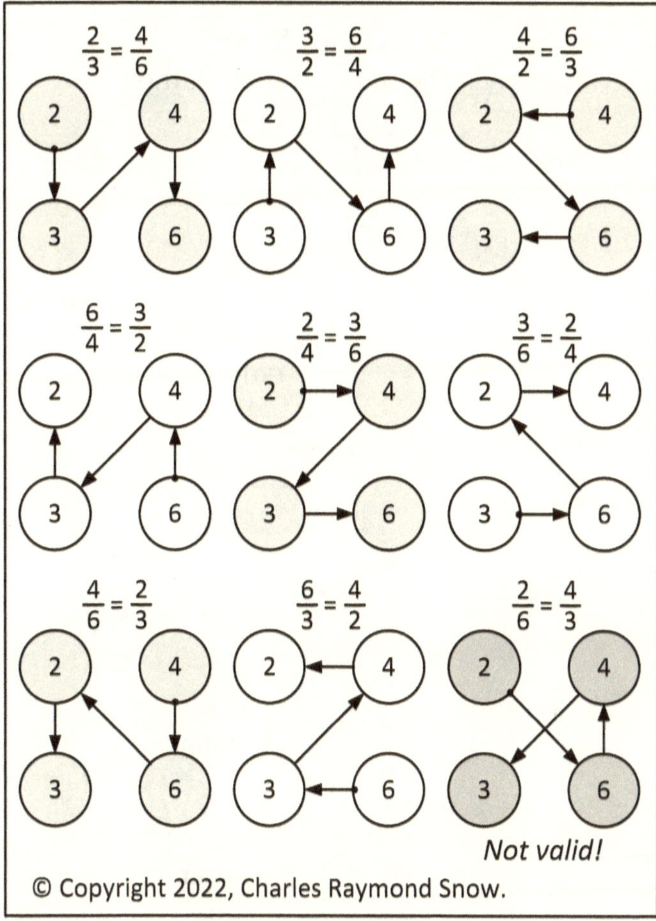

Figure 13: A Family of Proportions

One valid proportion gives rise to seven others.

It's conceivable that whenever a rapid serial display of four referent images occurs, the brain selects, from a polygon stack, unused vertices that represent the corresponding objects and actuates the connections that link them together.

The resulting neural structure constitutes a dispositional representation. Whenever it's invoked, it causes each vertex to signal the object pyramid to which it's connected (so that it can resurrect the corresponding image) and simultaneously signals the next vertex in the sequence (so that it can follow suit.) The net result is that the brain's owner perceives the four referents in quick succession and interprets the sequence as an analogy.

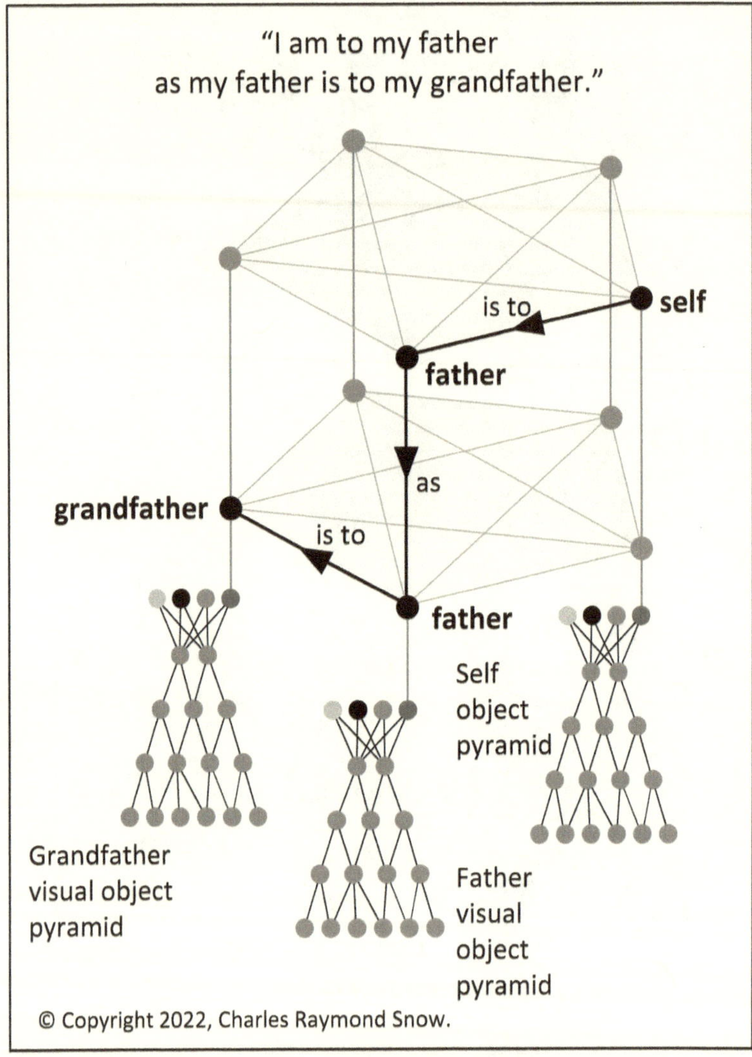

Figure 14: The Neural Representation of a Mean Analogy

A mean analogy is one in which the second and third elements are identical.

It's permissible for the second and third elements of an explicit analogy to be identical, as in, "I am to my father as my father is to my grandfather," assuming that only the patrilineal line is considered. Such an inference is called a mean analogy.

A mean analogy in which the first and third linkages are declarations of inclusion is called a syllogism. For instance, "John is a man, and a man is mortal." (This is an abbreviation of "John is included in the class of men, and men are included in the class of mortals.") This syllogism, when activated, is tantamount to inferring that John is mortal. Syllogisms are essential not only to inductive reasoning, but also to designing cascades of logic gates. (A logic gate is an electronic component that makes decisions by combining multiple binary inputs into a single binary output.)

Mean analogies can be linked together, as in "I am to my father as my father is to my grandfather, and my father is to my grandfather as my grandfather is to my great-grandfather," again assuming that only the patrilineal line is considered. A neural representation of this chain of analogies is illustrated in Figure 15. Invoking this chain is tantamount to inferring that, "I am to my father as my grandfather is to my great-grandfather."

(The diagonal link in Figure 15 between the second and third polygons implies the existence of a combinatorial explosion of connections between consecutive polygons. We'll ignore this complication.)

It's conceivable that the overall architecture of a chain of reasoning is a linked sequence of mean analogies. What makes it possible to assemble such a chain on the fly, even if it's relatively long, is that the required neural infrastructure already exists, and that only three connections need to be actuated in order to represent one analogy.

ς

The human species belongs to a taxonomic tribe of human-like apes, called hominins, that originated roughly after chimpanzees diverged from other primates. The Hominins include not only us, but also 20 other anthropoidal species, such as Homo habilis, Homo erectus, and Homo neanderthalensis.

Long before hominins acquired the ability to conduct formal inferential thinking, their ability to assemble sequences of mean analogies made possible a unique behavior called tracking.

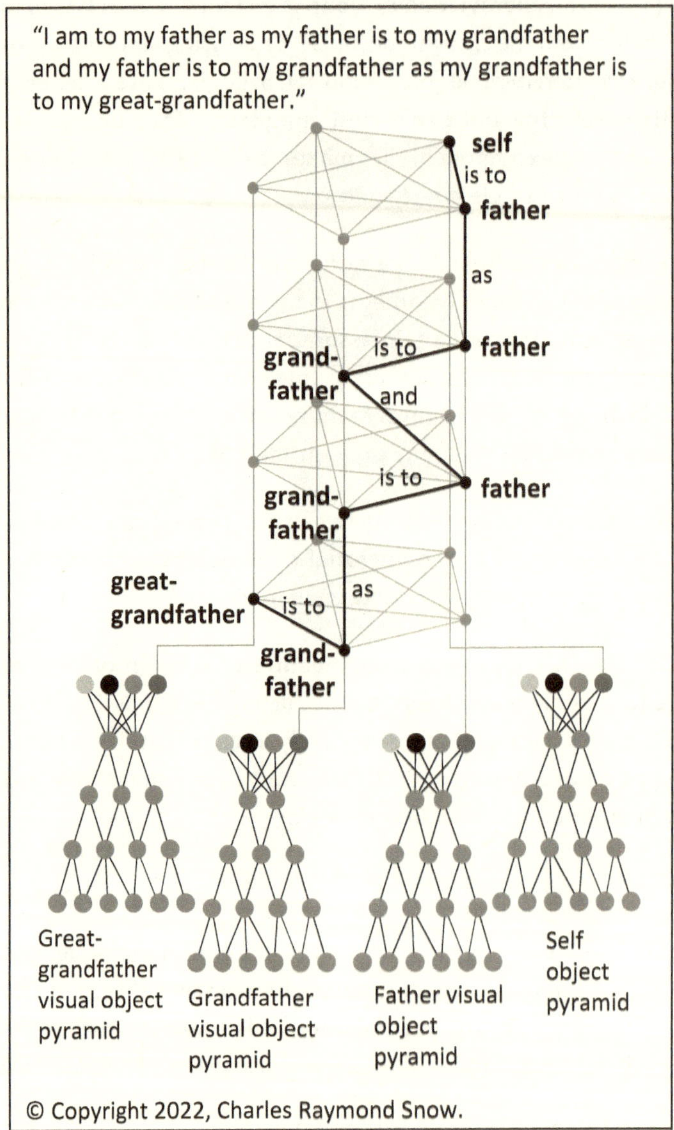

Figure 15: The Neural Representation
of a Chain of Analogies

Mean analogies can be linked together sequentially.

Tracking is the process of following the spoor of an animal. In the interest of simplicity, let's assume that the footprints that are to be followed are those of a biped, such as an ostrich. In order to be capable of tracking such an animal, a hunter must be able to perceive that the first footprint bears the same relationship to the second as the second does to the third, and so on. Absent this perception, a spoor is nothing more than an uninteresting bunch of depressions in the ground.

(In order for the hunter to track the animal, his brain must selectively ignore that the left and right footprints are slightly different, and that each footprint is offset to the left or right with respect to its predecessor. This illustrates that, occasionally, it's beneficial to its owner for the brain to selectively ignore sensory inputs.)

In evolution, few adaptations are as significant as those that increase an animal's ability to obtain food. Tracking transformed our ancestors from gatherers of sustenance in the forest to pursuers of prey on the plains. Because only hominins were able to follow the track of an animal, they became the sole occupants of a new ecological niche. As forest gatherers, they had had many competitors; as savannah trackers, they had none.

The ability of hominins to follow a chain of footprints probably improved their ability to construct a chain of ideas; constructing a chain of ideas is a type of nonverbal thinking; such thinking is a prerequisite for speech.

§

Some 17,000 years ago, a human drew superbly executed likenesses of aurochs, horses, and deer on the walls of a cavern in southwestern France. Such astonishing art probably was an outcome of a much earlier event, in which one of our ancestors, who could hunt by following a series of footprints, conceived of a long, narrow, continuous sequence. Such a concept is called a line. Without the ability to conceive lines, humans would never have painted the exquisite scenes in the Lascaux cave, and civilization, which relies heavily on drawings and diagrams, would never have evolved.

§

One of the principal forms of thinking is internal storytelling. The tales that we tell ourselves are the main cognitive instruments by which we understand the world; they consequently have a profound influence on our behavior.

Chapter 16: Autobiography, Storytelling, and the Brain

Whenever we think of storytelling among primitive people, we're likely to imagine an elder sitting by a campfire recounting a legend to a rapt audience of youngsters; but stories can be told to an entirely different audience in an entirely different way: a story can be told to oneself, silently, wordlessly, by imagining a series of pictures instead of speaking a series of words.

It's not surprising that the brain is receptive to stories; neurons and assemblies of neurons are vectorial structures that connect sequentially so that decision odysseys can flow through them; but sequence, direction, and flow also are fundamental properties of stories. This fortuitous similarity makes it easy for the brain's owner to understand something that's expounded within the context of a story, but hard to understand something that isn't; in other words, uniquely among neural artifacts, a story can serve as both a repository for knowledge and a context for understanding it. [130]

The most important story that an animal knows is its own biography. It's especially important to social species, because, in order for a social animal to interact prudently with a conspecific, it must first consider the cumulative effects of past interactions between itself and the other individual. By reexamining the numerous encounters that it's had with others, the animal effectively constructs an internal autobiography.

In earlier chapters, a way by which the brain might internalize, store, and recall a sequence of events was suggested. This speculative mechanism is further explored in the following paragraphs.

§

Suppose that a man who's attending a party recounts to the other guests an incident that took place on the preceding day:

> Butch, William, and I were sitting on a park bench at the
> zoo eating vanilla ice cream cones that we'd just bought
> at the concession stand, when suddenly a baboon who'd
> gotten loose charged at us, intent on stealing our ice creams.
> William retreated immediately, and initially, so did I.
> However, a moment later, having wrapped my arm around
> Butch's shoulder for moral support (Butch is pretty big,) I
> threatened the baboon, hoping to scare him off. The baboon
> threatened me back, so, I again sought Butch's support. This
> time, he stood up and we both threatened the baboon. The
> baboon retreated, but a moment later, he reached out and
> tried to slap me; so, eventually, I gave up and retreated,
> myself.

As the events that constitute this incident actually were taking place, the
narrator's inherently self-centered brain perceived them strictly as binary
social transactions in which he was the principal protagonist. Consequently,
it had to parse the incident into a sequence of alternating inbound and
outbound effectors. This could only be achieved by serializing events that, in
reality, were happening concurrently; and by interjecting transitional words,
such as "and then," "and also," and "so then."

Many details of the incident (that the companions were sitting on a bench,
for instance,) were considered by the narrator's brain to be nonessential; so,
it didn't record them. This means that the narrator confabulated them on
the fly while he was telling the story. Such unpremeditated interpolations
are common in ordinary discourse and, despite their possibly being false,
usually do no harm.

Having been transformed according to these caveats, the narrative may have
gone something like this:

> Ice cream is bought by me, and also Butch buying ice cream
> is seen by me, and also William buying ice cream is seen
> by me, so then me eat ice cream, and then baboon charges
> at me, and also baboon charging at Butch is seen by me,
> and also baboon charging at William is seen by me, and
> also William retreating from baboon is seen by me, so then
> me retreat from baboon, and also me embrace Butch, and

> also me threaten baboon, and then baboon threatens me, so
> then me embrace Butch, and also me see Butch threatening
> baboon, and also me threaten baboon, and then baboon
> retreats from me, and also baboon slaps at me, so then me
> retreat from baboon.

By so transforming the story, the narrator's brain has rendered it compatible with a neural polygon stack. Figure 16 depicts such a structure, within which the story is represented by a linked sequence of vertices. (In the interest of simplicity, only one ice cream is represented.) If the stack were to possess a sufficient number of platters to record every significant episode of the narrator's life, it could serve as the neural repository of his personal autobiography; let's assume that such a structure does, in fact, exist, and that it does, indeed, fulfill this role.

Although the Figure suggests that the story is internalized as a single continuous chain, it's actually internalized as a sequence of four binary transactions. (In the Figure, as well as in the transformed text, transactions are separated by "and then" pseudo-predicates, and their inbound and outbound halves are separated by "so then" pseudo-predicates.)

The inbound half of the first transaction is exceptional in three ways:

1. It comprises three inbound effectors, due to the fact that three unitary actions occur concurrently.

2. Because inbound effectors must have the self object as their recipient, the three predicates ("is bought by," "is seen by," and "is seen by," respectively) are expressed in the passive voice.

3. Because in the second and third effectors, "is seen by" serves as the predicate, and "me" serves as the recipient, the actions, "Butch buying ice cream," and, "William buying ice cream," respectively, serve as the initiators.

ξ

Besides functioning as a repository for the story, the linked sequence of vertices in the polygon stack also serves as a dispositional representation for retelling it; whenever the representation is invoked, it activates the vertices that it comprises consecutively; in so doing, it serially resurrects the images of the corresponding referents.

It's instructive to trace, vertex by vertex, the sensory effects that are produced whenever the dispositional representation is invoked. In the interest of brevity, we'll consider only the first transaction.

The dispositional representation launches this transaction by activating the topmost ice cream vertex, which reacts by activating the request neuron of the visual object pyramid that represents the ice cream. The activation of the request neuron sets off a cascade that reconstructs the visual object. This causes the narrator briefly to see a vanilla ice cream cone.

The reconstruction of the visual object triggers the reconstruction of the corresponding lexical object, which causes the narrator briefly to hear the term, "ice cream," and thereby enables him to recite it.

Next, via the "is bought by" connection, the dispositional representation activates the second vertex, which is labeled "me." This vertex reacts by activating the request neuron of the self object pyramid.

The activation of this neuron sets off a cascade that transforms the unified feeling of the body into an explicit awareness of the self. This causes the narrator to realize that he, himself, is the other protagonist of the unitary action, and prompts him to so inform his audience.

The activation of the first two vertices constitutes the execution of the first effector; because this effector is inbound, the brain realizes that the ice cream has performed a unitary action upon the self. But what particular action was it?

At first glance, Figure 16 would seem to provide an answer: above the connection that links the "ice cream" vertex to the "me" vertex are the words, "is bought by." But although in the Figure, the connection is labeled, within the narrator's brain, it isn't; the brain has to figure out for itself what the ice cream did to the narrator. (Actually, it was the narrator who did something to the ice cream: he bought it; but because an inbound effector must have the self object as its recipient, the brain casts the ice cream as the initiator.)

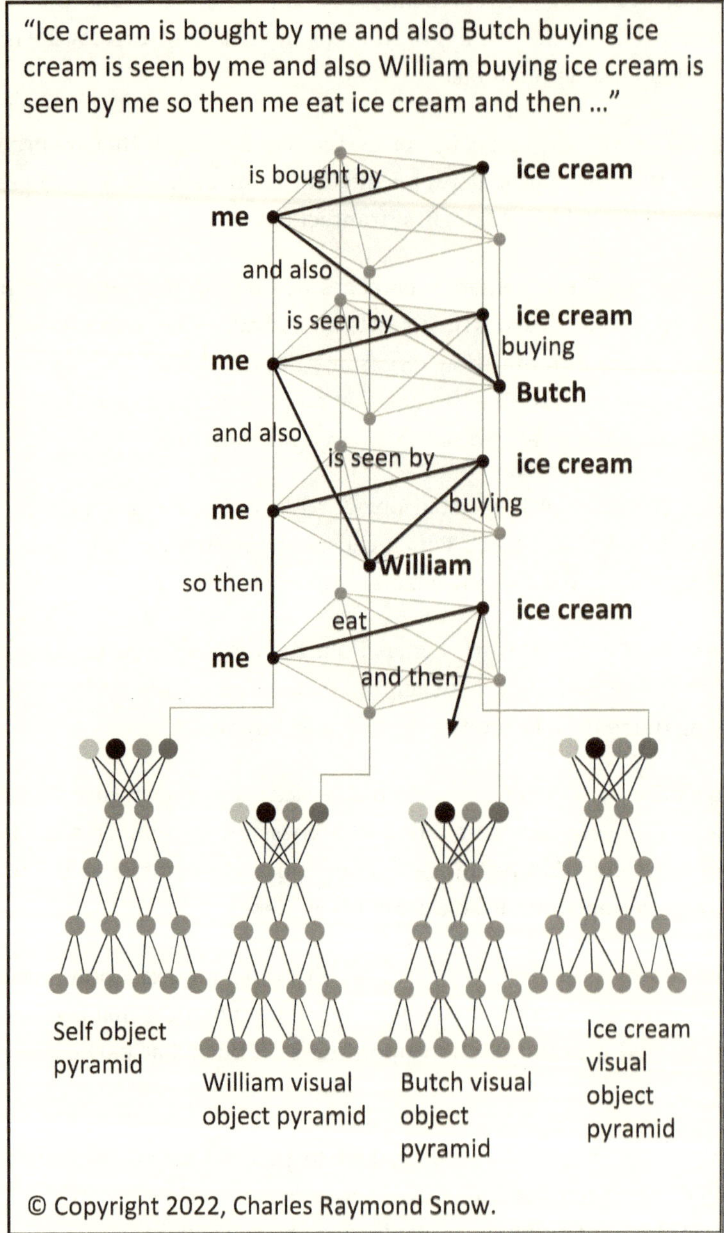

Figure 16: The Neural Representation of a Story

A story can be represented by a linked sequence of vertices within a neural polygon stack.

We don't entirely know how the brain decides on the correct interpretation of an action predicate. Nevertheless, it seems likely that, in many instances, it can make this determination solely on the basis of contextual data, such as the identities of the initiator and the recipient, proximate sensory images, or concurrent actions (that are more easily deciphered) which are undertaken by others.

Sometimes, the first interpretation is shown, by subsequent events in the story, to be erroneous; under these circumstances, the brain selects another interpretation and completely forgets the former one; and the narrator, if he's honest, backpedals in order to revise his narrative. In the present case, we'll assume that the brain correctly identifies the first predicate, and thereby interprets the first effector as "Ice cream is bought by me."

Having executed the first effector, which is inbound, the dispositional representation now executes the second and third, which also are inbound.

Next, via the "so then" pseudo-predicate, the dispositional representation executes the outbound effector. The outbound effector has the same protagonists as the first inbound effector, namely "ice cream" and "me," except that their roles are reversed; so, the outbound action predicate is easily deciphered: within the context of the story, the only thing that the narrator is likely to do to the ice cream is to eat it.

Overall, as the dispositional representation activates one transaction after another and the narrator's brain confabulates to make them consistent, [131] the story emerges and ultimately clarifies.

§

It's instructive to imagine, at a rapid pace, the prominent sensory images that are invoked by the execution of the first five effectors:

1. A *picture* of ice cream; the *sound* of the words, "ice cream"; *an explicit awareness of the self.*

2. A *picture* of Butch; the *sound* of the name, "Butch"; a *picture* of ice cream; the *sound* of the words, "ice cream"; *an explicit awareness of the self.*

3. A *picture* of William; the *sound* of the name, "William"; a *picture* of ice cream; the *sound* of the words, "ice cream"; *an explicit awareness of the self.*

4. *An explicit awareness of the self;* a *picture* of ice cream; the *sound* of the words, "ice cream."

5. A *picture* of the baboon; the *sound* of the word, "baboon"; *an explicit awareness of the self.*

The execution of the first four effectors depicts a group of friends who are happily eating ice cream and engenders feelings of comradery and well-being; but the execution of the fifth depicts an aggressive baboon who's approaching rapidly and engenders a feeling of fear.

All of this suggests that a rough sketch of what happened can be cobbled together from nothing more than the objects, the order in which they appear, the sensations that they regenerate, the emotions and feelings that they re-engender, and a little confabulating. (None of these necessitates the use of words. This strongly suggests that the neural representation of a story is language-independent.) It's likely that most memories are reconstructed in this haphazard way; that they may not precisely reflect the actual events usually doesn't matter.

Unfortunately, sometimes it does. In a court of law, for instance, eyewitness testimony requires the witness to reconstruct past events from memory. But such testimony is notoriously unreliable because it's subject to many kinds of error. For example:

1. When the event transpired, the witness's brain may have perceived it incorrectly.

2. If the event was ambiguous, the brain may subsequently have reconstructed it incorrectly.

3. If it was frightening, the brain may have rewritten it so as to either understate, or overstate, the danger.

Such errors frequently result in the wrongful conviction of an innocent person.

ξ

A few days after the party, the narrator has a conversation with his wife, during which she mentions his friend, William, by name. Suddenly, a nearly complete reenactment of the incident at the zoo springs into the narrator's conscious awareness.

How can the mere mention of a name trigger the recollection of an incident?

A possible mechanism is illustrated in Figure 17. When the narrator's wife utters William's name, the narrator's brain reflexively selects an unused lexical auditory object pyramid and begins to objectify the sound of the name, "William." In the process, it produces a digest of the sound in its identification neuron, and, via a recognition polygon, distributes the digest to all of the other lexical pyramids.

Among them is the pyramid that originally objectified the sound of William's name. (That the narrator may know of several men named William is a complication that we'll ignore.) Whenever this pyramid receives a digest from the recognition polygon, it regenerates its own digest, and the narrator's brain compares the former with the latter.

In this instance, the brain determines that the degree of similarity between the two digests is sufficient for them to be considered identical; so, it activates the pyramid's request neuron; this triggers the reconstruction of the corresponding lexical object, and thereby causes the narrator to hear William's name.

The reconstruction of the lexical object, via an apex-to-apex connection, triggers the reconstruction of the corresponding visual object, which, in turn, triggers the reconstruction of the appropriate facial visual object. This causes the narrator to see William's face.

But, as the story in Chapter 9 suggests, merely seeing William's face isn't sufficient to cause the narrator to recognize the person to whom his wife is referring.

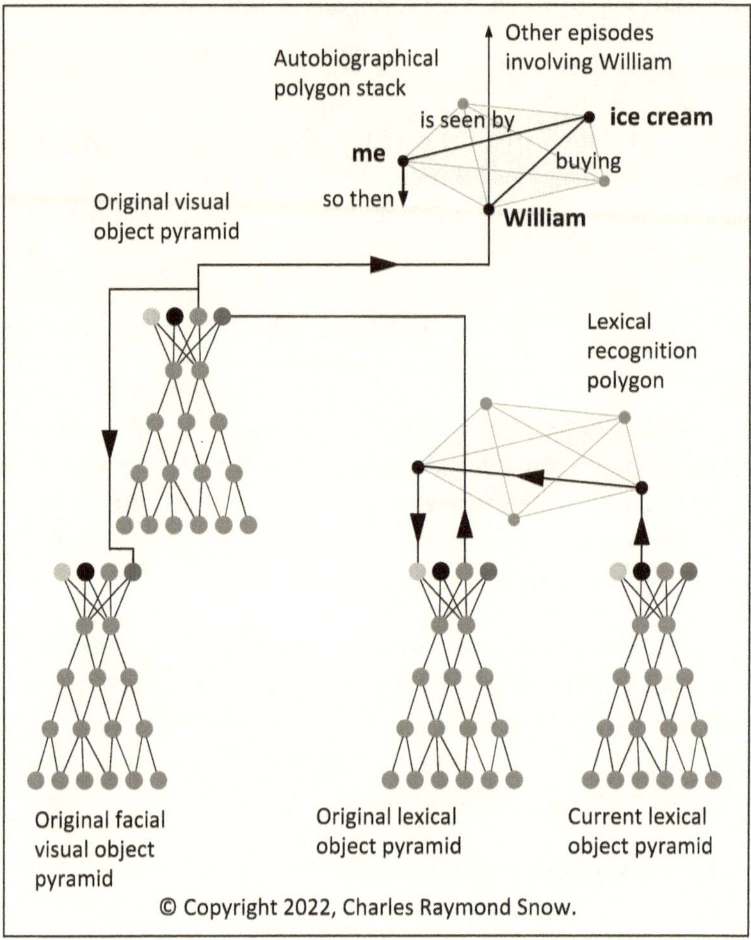

Figure 17: A Mechanism for Triggering a Recollection

The mention of William's name sets off a chain of events within the narrator's brain that partially replays the incident that occurred at the zoo.

However, when the lexical object pyramid (that originally objectified the sound of William's name) regenerates the sound, it also induces the amygdala to generate an "Aha!" This causes the narrator to realize that the person that's being discussed is his friend, William.

Finally, via the visual object's response neuron, which connects to all of the vertices that represent William in the autobiographical polygon stack, the brain kicks off partial reenactments of the corresponding episodes. It's conceivable that as it does so, by making use of contextual data, the brain suppresses the reenactment of every episode except the one about the zoo.

§

A person who undergoes a life-threatening experience can have a reaction that's epitomized by the words, "I saw my life flashing before me." An autobiographical neural polygon stack affords to the brain a mechanism by which it can create this effect.

It's conceivable that extreme fear causes the self object pyramid to activate (via its response neuron) all of the stack vertices that represent the self, each of which, when activated, launches a partial reenactment of the corresponding episode.

But every episode in the stack contains at least one such vertex; consequently, every episode is reenacted, and the brain, hampered by its owner's panic, is unable to suppress any of them.

§

We now come to one of the most contentious issues in science: language; in particular, spoken, verbal language. How could so complex a behavior have arisen via evolution and natural selection? And how do children learn so rapidly to speak? These questions famously have been investigated by Noam Chomsky. In the next chapter, we'll see that topographic psychology suggests credible answers.

Chapter 17: Evolutionary Antecedents of Language

Topographic psychology proposes that the behavioral suite of an animal species has a phylogenetic history; in other words, the behaviors of any animal must have evolved from the behaviors of its ancestors. In some cases, evidence of a behavior has been preserved in the fossil record. For instance, the earliest use of fire by hominins is being determined by analysis of archaic charcoal, bones, and tools that are associated with presumptive ancient hearths. But for the most part, conduct doesn't fossilize.

Of all characteristic human behaviors, language has been the most puzzling. How could so complex a phenomenon have arisen via evolution and natural selection? A credible explanation should identify a succession of behaviors, beginning in the single-celled ancestor of all extant living things and ending in humans, that could have led to speech. Because conduct rarely fossilizes, such a list would certainly be incomplete; nevertheless, an attempt to assemble one might prove to be instructive.

The overall structure of the cranial brain was shaped by four evolutionary watersheds, each of which gave rise to new kinds of behaviors. [132-133] Living as a lifelong member of an extended family necessitated the conducting of a kind of behavior called a binary social transaction. Primates engaged in such interactions via a combination of body language, facial expressions, vocalizations, and gestures. The increase in the complexity of their social lives was accompanied by a commensurate increase in their intelligence, which, in turn, enabled hominins to hunt by following a linked sequence of footprints and to reason by constructing a linked sequence of ideas. Subsequently, the descent of the voice box to its current position in the throat enabled humans to express such ideas linguistically. [134]

All of this suggests that spoken language was the outcome of a succession that includes the following behaviors. (As it happens, this list also enumerates elements of the hidden infrastructure that enables children to so rapidly learn to speak.) [135]

1. Maintaining homeostasis via secretion and the bloodstream.

2. Maintaining homeostasis via neurotransmission and the nervous system.

3. Executing fixed action patterns (such as reflexes, feelings, and emotions.)

4. Creating visual objects that represent external referents.

5. Creating auditory objects that represent sounds.

6. Creating connections between objects.

7. Constructing an explicit self. [136]

8. Performing voluntary actions.

9. Creating avatars that represent other family members. [137]

10. Conducting binary social transactions through body language, vocalizations, gestures, and facial expressions.

11. Constructing sequences, analogies, and linked sequences of mean analogies.

12. Assembling linked sequences of ideas.

13. Creating lexical auditory objects (words) that represent external referents.

14. Assembling linked sequences of words.

15. Speaking in a grammatical verbal language.

Because lexical objects, instead of being auditory, can be gestural, none of the items in this list precludes a human conversing with another kind of anthropoid. [138-139]

ş

The cardinal properties of spoken language are vocabulary, grammar, and semantics: [140-141]

1. Vocabulary is a mapping between external referents and internal lexical auditory objects that are called words. If the referent is a tangible entity, the corresponding object is referred to as its name. (For instance, in the English language, the name that corresponds to a seat that has four legs and a back is the lexical auditory object whose pronunciation is "chair.")

2. Grammar is a set of familial rules that prescribe which kinds of words may adjoin one another, and in what order, within a sentence.

3. Semantics are the meanings that one interlocutor can glean from the grammatical expression, by another interlocutor, of words from an appropriate vocabulary.

§

In evolution, one adaptation can serve multiple purposes. It's generally understood that spoken language improves communication between humans; but it also improves communication with oneself (otherwise known as thinking,) and, moreover, increases its speed.

But what is it about language that promotes this acceleration? For the purpose of answering this question, data retrieval in a computer can serve as a useful analog.

In order to quickly retrieve a record from a data file, a computer program can employ a technique called hashing. If hashing isn't available, then the program typically must search for the record by scanning the file sequentially; a process that's extremely slow by comparison.

In order to be susceptible to being retrieved by hashing, a record must previously have been stored in the file at a location whose address can be derived (via a mathematical algorithm) from a data item that's a part of the record, and whose value is commonly known. For example, if the record contains the personal data of an employee, the designated data item might be the employee's name.

Subsequently, the program can retrieve the record by re-deriving the address from the employee's name, and then accessing the data that begins at that address.

In an analogous way, a languaged human can quickly recall the visible appearance of a referent by speaking its name (either aloud or silently.) What makes this possible is the presence, in his or her brain, of a lexical auditory object pyramid that encodes the sound of the referent's name, a visual object pyramid that encodes the referent's visible appearance, and a bidirectional apex-to-apex connection that links them to each other.

By way of example, suppose that you're briefly shown a flash card bearing the equation, "$\mu = \varphi\lambda+\zeta$," and are directed to shut your eyes for ten seconds and then write the equation on a piece of paper. This is a trivial task if you have a photographic memory, but what if you don't?

If you're like most people, when you see the flash card, you laboriously commit the contours of the unfamiliar symbols to memory, and, subsequently, laboriously write them down.

But if you happen to be familiar with the Greek alphabet, when you see the flash card, you silently recite to yourself the sentence, "Mu equals Phi Lamda plus Zeta," (repeatedly, if necessary,) until ten seconds have elapsed, and then effortlessly write out the corresponding equation.

If, indeed, you're able to do this, it's because your brain contains visual object pyramids that represent the glyphs, "μ," "φ," "λ," and "ζ," lexical auditory object pyramids that represent the phonemes, "Mew," Fye," "Lamda," and "Zātah," and bidirectional connections that link the former to the latter. So, when you see the equation, the image of each letter automatically brings to mind the sound of the corresponding phoneme; and when you speak the equation, the sound of each letter automatically brings to mind the image of the corresponding glyph.

All of this suggests that the principal benefit of speech isn't that it improves communication with others, but rather that it speeds communication with oneself.

ζ

The worldwide community of countries occasionally is referred to as the family of nations. If this metaphor is fitting, then in order to understand the relationships between nation-states, it may be useful first to understand the social dynamics of the family.

Chapter 18: Family Social Dynamics and the Internet

The internal social dynamics of the extended family have had a profound influence upon the evolution of the brain. [142] Why should this be so? In order to answer this question, the Internet can be used as an analog.

The Internet is a large network of computers that conducts client-server transactions. If an Internet computer malfunctions, it safely can be taken off-line without compromising the integrity of the whole network. New computers can be linked in without much fanfare. Multiple tasks that are being performed by one computer can be distributed among and performed by others; conversely, multiple tasks that are being performed by other computers can be consolidated and performed by one.

This is a pretty good description of family activities, too. The commodities that are exchanged during intrafamilial transactions are the necessities of life; chief among these are safety from aggression by others, sexual intercourse, companionship, food, water, shelter, and medical care. [143-144]

It's generally believed that the complexity of the Internet is proportional to the number of computers that it contains; but that isn't the case: because the Internet enables one computer to interact with another, its true complexity is proportional to the maximum number of pairs of computers that can be formed within it. Likewise, because intrafamilial transactions are binary, a reasonable measure of a family's social complexity is the maximum number of pairs of members that can be formed within it.

Consider, for instance, a family of four who, whenever they gather for dinner, shake hands with each other exactly once. Member one shakes hands with members two, three, and four. Then, in order to avoid shaking hands with the same person twice, member two shakes hands with members three and four. Then, for the same reason, member three shakes hands with member four. The total number of handshakes, therefore, is 6.

By way of comparison, imagine that their next-door neighbors, a family of eight, also practices the traditional dinnertime handshake. In their case, the total number of handshakes is 28.

Now suppose that over a period of 90 years, due to marriages, childbirths, and adoptions, the population of this family increases from 8 to 100. Then, at dinnertime, the family will have to perform a total of 4,950 handshakes (which means that dinner will probably be cold by the time they sit down.)

This disproportionate increase in the number of pairs that can be selected from a given population is easily overlooked or underestimated; but, for the purpose of understanding behavior, it's very revealing: for it makes manifest the usually invisible complexity of animal social life.

In the present case, although the number of family members has multiplied by a factor of 12, the number of handshakes has multiplied by a factor of 176; so have the numbers of many other interactions.

Very likely, the multiplicity of social transactions that an animal must conduct if it is to live as a good citizen of an extended family demands a bigger, smarter brain; [145] a notion that's partially supported by the fact that all intelligent vertebrate species are highly social.

A social bond that's sustained via repeated transactions commonly is called a relationship. In order to govern effectively, the leader of an extended family must maintain many relationships. But children only need to maintain a few, [146] because from their perspective, the only ones that matter are those that are between themselves and their closest relatives and friends; nevertheless, because one of them may someday become the leader, their brains must have the capacity to attend to many.

§

Social life within the extended family consists of an ongoing sequence of binary transactions that requires a continual exchange of verbal or nonverbal messages. At first glance, this constant dialoging may seem unstructured; yet there must be a system that enables members to distinguish between messages that are significant and messages that aren't. How do they make this distinction?

Sometimes it's easier to explain something by describing its opposite; in the present case, what's needed is a network in which all messages are of equal import; an Ethernet network has this property.

Ethernet technology has undergone several revisions. In the interest of simplicity, we'll consider only the original version, in which a set of computers that are relatively close together are connected directly to a coaxial cable, and each message is encoded as a sequence of voltages called a packet. Within such a network, all messages are considered to be equally important. Under these circumstances, there's nothing to prevent two computers from attempting to send messages at exactly the same time. Whenever this occurs, the voltage packets, as they propagate electrically along the cable, encounter and interfere with each other, and are thereby rendered indecipherable. (Modern Ethernet networks rarely experience such packet collisions.) Because the stymied computers are electrically connected to the same cable, both are aware that their packets have been destroyed, but neither knows the identity of the other. What should they do? If they transmit again, they may get another collision.

The solution is for both to back off for a short time of random duration, and then try again. They may need to repeat this procedure several times, but eventually, they'll select different back-off times, and the packets no longer will collide.

Within the dangerous world of animal survival, however, it's not prudent to rely on retransmission as a way of ensuring the delivery of a message. If, during a crisis, a critical signal isn't received and understood immediately by its intended audience, a death can result. Consequently, under normal survival pressures, families that possess poor communication systems eventually are eliminated by natural selection.

For the sake of argument, imagine a family whose communication style is similar to that of an Ethernet network, and suppose that, suddenly, the family is confronted with a mortal danger. What happens? At precisely the moment that clarity is needed, many members signal each other, and their messages collide. They then have to back off and try again; moreover, because of the confusion, they may have to try again repeatedly. This consumes precious time and increases the likelihood that someone will die.

Therefore, in regard to surviving mortal dangers, universal equality is counterproductive; what's needed is a system of authority and communication that's simple enough to be understood and utilized by everyone. Such systems typically are based on status.

Within every extended family, there's a status system in which each member is assigned a rank, and individuals of high rank have greater power than others. [147] In the simplest systems, status is based upon raw physical strength, and the family is dominated by an alpha male to whom everyone looks for leadership in an emergency; the other members are arrayed beneath him in one or more subordinate ranks. At first glance, this would seem to preclude democracy; but the social dynamics of the extended family are subtle and complex, and, in practice, absolute despotism is uncommon, and, sometimes, the family member who ascends to the topmost post is a female.

A family member can improve their status by mating someone of higher rank, by committing an act of valor, or by performing some other beneficial act. But they can lose their social standing by being widowed, by failing to share food with other family members, or by doing something else that's detrimental. Physical beauty usually enhances status; on the other hand, possession of high status often compensates for being homely.

So essential to the family's survival is the status system that some species, orangutans, for instance, have evolved anatomical differences between males of different ranks; dominant orangutan males have larger cheek pads.

It isn't sufficient, however, for family members to recognize such cues; they also must understand their meanings and accept the authority that they imply. Nothing will enrage an alpha male more than another male who ignores, or is unaware of, the dominant male's status and fails to treat him with deference.

No matter how small in population, regardless of whether its members belong to the same family or are an ad hoc collection of strangers, a group of social animals can't function effectively without a leader. This is as true of humans as it is of hyenas. Even in a gang that consists of two individuals, invariably, one is dominant and the other, submissive.

§

Whenever a familial transaction takes place, each participant must know what actions are appropriate. The easiest way to achieve this is to get everybody to internalize the same set of rules. But if the species is highly social, the protocols of the extended family can be many and complex. How is this large body of knowledge organized? To answer this question, yet another feature of the Internet can be utilized as an analog.

In order to enable computers of different types to interact with one another, the communications software on all computers that access the Internet must conform to a large set of rules. For the sake of efficiency and tractability, these rules are partitioned into layers. Whenever someone uses an Internet service, such as on-line shopping, searching, or social networking, he or she provides information to the topmost layer; that is to say, to a program that's operating in accordance with the rules of the topmost layer. The program encodes the user's input as a service request message and passes it to the layer directly below, which transforms it according to rules that govern that layer. The message continues to be passed downward, layer by layer, until, at the bottommost, it's transformed into a sequence of voltages (or, less commonly, a sequence of light pulses) that's placed onto the cable that connects the computer to the Internet.

For the sake of simplicity, each layer focuses on only the tasks that it, alone, can perform well, and interacts only with the layer that's directly above or directly below. Such an ensemble of communications layers is called a protocol stack.

When the message arrives at the server, it traverses the layers in reverse order; each layer translates it into the appropriate dialect and conveys it to the next highest layer. As a result, the data that arrives at the topmost layer on the server is identical to the data that was dispatched from the topmost layer on the client; yet none of the layers, on either the client or the server, is aware of the message's odyssey down one protocol stack, across the network, and up another. [148]

Now, let's consider an extended family of humans. A family is composed of members who differ in gender, age, and status. In order to promote effective dialoging amidst this diversity, intrafamilial communications are governed by a large number of rules that reside within the brains of all family members. For the sake of efficiency and tractability, these rules, like the rules of the Internet, are partitioned into layers. [149]

In the same way that an Internet message originates in the topmost layer of the client's protocol stack, a spoken sentence originates in the imaging shell of the initiator's brain. The sentence then propagates downward to the family shell, where it's modulated according to family rules concerning courtesy, empathy, and respect for authority. The family shell is able to conduct this supervision by virtue of the presence in the brain, not only of the autobiographical self, which serves as a proxy for the owner of the brain, but also of avatars that represent the owner's relatives and friends, which serve as a proxy for the family. These virtual companions either approve or disapprove of the sentence that the imaging shell has concocted; in the latter case, they may modify the sentence to make it more acceptable; or, if it's egregiously inappropriate, they may suppress it altogether. (Colloquially, "If you can't say something nice, don't say nothing at all.")

The sentence then propagates downward into the self shell, which modifies it according to rules that are appropriate to that layer, and reformulates it in a way that renders it compatible with the next lowest layer.

When the sentence arrives at the primordial core, it's transformed into a sequence of fixed action patterns, each of which, when executed, engages the diaphragm, the lungs, the vocal cords, the tongue, and the mouth in order to produce a phoneme. The net result is to impose variations in pressure onto the air that surrounds the initiator; such variations are what we call sounds.

The sounds thus produced propagate through the air, through the recipient's auditory system, and into the primordial core of the recipient's brain, where they're transformed into a sequence of phonemes. The sequence then propagates upward through the next two layers, each of which incrementally elaborates it, so that, when it's forwarded to the imaging shell, it can be transformed back into a spoken sentence.

However, unlike an Internet message, which arrives at the server's top layer bearing data that's identical to that which was sent by the client, the sentence that's produced by the recipient's imaging shell isn't guaranteed to be identical to the sentence that was uttered by the initiator.

As the proto-sentence propagates upward through the recipient's brain, it's interpreted by each layer according to the state of the recipient's body. If the two interlocutors are getting along, the sentence is unlikely to be altered; but if, previous to the conversation, the recipient has become angry with the initiator (in other words, if the state of their body has swapped into the violence context,) he or she is likely to interpret each word in the most pessimistic way possible. Under these circumstances, as the sentence propagates upward through the recipient's brain, one of the layers is likely to alter it by changing its tone or by inserting, deleting, or replacing a word. The modified sentence may, thenceforth, possess a different meaning than the one that the initiator intended.

§

Members of a human family converse often. Among these many dialogs, those that are conducted with a senior family member are the most significant; for it's through such conversations that the family leadership influences everyone else. An individual can talk with a senior family member whether the latter is actually present or not; if present, the junior member conducts an external conversation with the senior; if not, the self object of the former conducts an internal conversation with an avatar that represents the latter; often, such internal conversations are conducted nonconsciously.

It's easy to underestimate the influence of an internal dialog with a senior family member; it carries the same authority as an external one. Such internal dialogs usually are launched involuntarily, and are conducted throughout the day, even if the junior member is alone, far away from the family homestead, or asleep. These internal conversations are the bedrock upon which shame, virtue, guilt, and the conscience are built. [150] It's not possible to understand a human's behavior without taking them into account.

Chapter 19: The Earliest Humans

Analysis of the human genome has revealed that all modern humans descended from people who lived approximately 50,000 years ago in central and southern Africa. [151] Very likely, these ancestors were members of an extant ethnic group called the bushmen. Although it's impossible to identify the founding members of any species, for the purpose of understanding behavior, it's useful to conceive that bushmen were the first true humans. Let's assume that this is so, and see where it leads.

The original human beings, the first African hominins who looked like us and behaved like us, had oriental eyes and yellow skin that was tanned to a copper brown. [152-154] The tops of their heads were sparsely covered by tightly curling hair. They were tall and slim, possessed efficient hearts and capacious lungs, and, on the average, lived 47 years. [155] They were social creatures whose extended families numbered as many as 150 souls. [156] The family was divided into groups and dispersed among camps that were located within the family territory.

The only animals that preyed upon them were leopards, [157] who typically hunted at night, and which the people defeated handily by sleeping around a communal fire in huts or lean-tos that they had fashioned from tree limbs and branches. They cooked food during the day and told stories at night. They had little need for privacy and little need for secrets.

The totality of their possessions consisted of a long digging stick, ostrich eggshells for carrying water, fire-making sticks, slings or bags for carrying things, a bone knife, and the clothes that they were wearing, which were exquisitely decorated with colored beads.

Their chief competitors were lions (a pride of lions and an extended family of humans required the same amount of meat per week); nevertheless, they treated the lions with respect. [158] They knew the properties of every local species of plant and tree and the behaviors of every local species of animal.

Figure 18: The Physical Appearance of the First Humans

It's likely that the original human beings had oriental eyes, yellow skin that was tanned to a copper brown, and tightly curling hair that sparsely covered the tops of their heads.

They ate the produce of more than 80 kinds of plants [159] and knew the locations of every source of water, nuts, edible roots, vegetables, and fruits within their territory. They were partial to honey and, from time to time, carried smoking branches into the trees and raided the hives. [160]

Their greatest satisfaction lay in dandling their children upon their knees. Their sole communion with the divine was to thank it for its bounty. Although they sometimes went hungry, they never starved. [161] They suffered neither famine nor disease. [162] Heart ailments were unknown; cancers rare. Built into their lifestyle were checks and balances that minimized conflict and aggression. Whenever necessary, justice was dispensed quickly, pragmatically, and unceremoniously. [163] Murder was uncommon; rape impossible. Wars were brutal, infrequent, and short. [164]

Figure 19: The First Humans Walked
and Ran Great Distances

Women frequently walked 14 miles in order to forage
for food; men routinely ran for 5 hours in order to chase
down an antelope.

Women regularly walked 14 miles in order to forage for food. [165] Typically, they gathered in small groups and left their encampments in the early morning. Each woman carried a digging stick made of dense wood and had two slings draped over her shoulders: one to carry ostrich eggshells that she had filled with drinking water and the other to carry her baby. In the late afternoon, after gathering food, she tied as many as 70 pounds of firewood into a bundle, slung it across her back, and carried the wood, the food, and her baby back to camp. [166]

Whenever a considerable amount of meat was needed, the men walked onto the savannah and searched until they found the hoofprints of a large antelope. [167] They followed the trail, sometimes over bare rock, until they could see the animal. [168] Then they ran toward it at a moderate pace. The antelope bolted and ran for about one minute, covering a distance of about one-quarter of a mile. Then it tired, sought shade, cooled its body by panting, and eventually recovered its strength. But invariably, the men found the antelope again. So, it ran again.

This could go on for as many as five or six hours, but eventually, the animal could no longer move. With its legs splayed, with its body temperature soaring, it stood panting heavily in a vain attempt to cool down. The men, because of their upright posture, naked skin, and sweat glands, and because of their ability to take more than one breath per stride, had no such problem. Calmly, they approached the antelope, placed their hands on its head, asked forgiveness, and thanked the animal for its body. Then, one man cupped his hands over the antelope's nostrils so that it couldn't breathe, and within minutes, it died. The only tool they carried was a bone knife. They knelt, butchered the body quickly, slung pieces over their shoulders, and walked home.

§

We are today beset by threats that are widespread, complex, and deadly: larger and more frequent hurricanes, tornados, and wildfires; decimation of oceanic fish stocks; perpetual warfare; and proliferation of nuclear weapons. None of these problems existed 400 years ago.

It's possible that human progress, as it's usually conceived, is now, or soon will be, at an impasse. If so, a reasonable salutary course of action would be to deliberately regress to a simpler way of life. But every known attempt to do so, or to construct a utopian society from scratch, has ended in failure.

What's needed is a viable example; a lifestyle that's known to have existed and that served its people well. In view of the longevity of the bushmen's way of life, perhaps we should consider the example of the earliest humans. Their success suggests that we were designed by Nature, not to be great thinkers, but rather to regularly walk, and periodically run, great distances; to eat many different kinds of plants, supplemented by weekly doses of cooked meat; [169] to live in small communities in which everyone knows everyone else; and to conduct uncomplicated lives that value strength, endurance, courage, and devotion to family.

Chapter 20: The Divine

The physical universe contains three kinds of things: matter, forces, and laws. Outside of physics and cosmology, neither matter nor forces are ever conceptually consolidated; but the laws of nature are, and sometimes are referred to as God. [170] So, purely for the sake of argument, let's make the assumption that the union of all natural laws constitutes something transcendent, and see where it leads.

It's difficult for humans to resist naming anything that we perceive; so, strictly within the confines of this chapter, let's agree to call this transcendent referent "the authority."

What are its characteristics?

- The authority exists, not in a separate dimension, but in the real physical universe. It isn't invisible and can be seen simply by demonstrating one of its laws.

- The authority doesn't have a body, and, consequently, it isn't a life-form; but if it did have a body, and if that body was human-like, then its left arm might be relativity, its right arm evolution, and its left big toe the number, pi. (The ratio of a circle's circumference to its diameter.)

- Everything that the authority does consumes time; consequently, it doesn't bring things into existence instantaneously. It has never been observed to do anything at a speed that's greater than 186,000 miles per second (the speed of light in a vacuum.)

- The authority has never been known to break one of its own laws; things that it's been observed to do that, at the time, seemed inexplicable, sometime later were found to have an explanation.

- The authority doesn't know anything and doesn't think. To know and to think require a physical body, a brain, an internal world model, a community of conspecifics, and a verbal or nonverbal language. But the authority has none of these. Why, for instance, would it need a world model when it's got the real thing at its disposal?

- The authority favors no one; to the authority, all of its creations, living and inanimate, have equal worth. To ask why bad things happen to good people presumes that there are people who aren't good; but the impartiality of the authority is absolute; in its eyes, none of its creations are bad.

- In the face of danger, all that any of us can do is to try to stay alive for as long as possible; for it's through the struggle of each of its creatures to survive that the authority manages the well-being of all.

- The authority produces right action, not by threatening punishment or promising reward, but by encoding the rules of right behavior in the genomes of its creatures; [171] and by endowing social species with instincts that generally prevent murder.

- The authority isn't omnipotent: it shares power with the laws of chance. Indeed, the engine that drives the molecular interactions within a living cell is the rapid and random movement of its contents by virtue of heat. [172]

These ideas raise a significant question: If there is, indeed, something transcendent, what is the proper attitude that a thinking being should have toward it?

Very likely, in the earliest humans, it consisted of respect and gratitude; nothing else was needed. As to whether so simple a religion could have served them well, one should consider that they were stronger and healthier than us; that they had no fears; and that their way of life has survived, essentially unchanged, from 50,000 years ago until the present day. [173-174]

Chapter 21: What Can Go Wrong?

Topographic psychology doesn't prescribe specific solutions to large-scale societal problems. It does, however, present little-known facts that can illuminate acts of murder, genocide, terrorism, and war. Such events largely are caused by a relatively small set of pathological behaviors:

1. legal fictions

2. follies of two

3. war by proxy

4. the amok mindset

5. psychopathy

A review of pertinent events in recent history will help to elucidate them.

§

One of the benefits of verbal language is the capacity to create useful legal fictions: false ideas that are held to be true because they're convenient and acceptable to many people. (The idea that paper currency has value, for instance, is a legal fiction.) For the purpose of understanding behavior, the significance of legal fictions is that, despite their falseness, they become ensconced as facts in their adherents' world models.

There's compelling evidence that humans are adapted to living in communities of about 150 people; to occupying a large communal proprietary territory; [175-177] and to walking and running great distances. But in the industrial west, for the most part, people lead sedentary lives, in apartments or in houses on small plots of land, and in nuclear families.

Because they're cut off from their natural physical and social environments, [178] only an anthology of legal fictions can unite them. Under these circumstances, a legal fiction can become pathological.

That the spread of communism was a mortal danger to the United States was a widely held idea among Americans after World War Two. The American government adopted it as gospel; an unquestioned truth that thenceforth informed all aspects of the foreign policy of the United States. Accordingly, the emergence of communism in any country, no matter how small in territory or population, was perceived as a threat.

But in reality, communism and its chief exponent, the Soviet Union, were much weaker than they appeared. Although its nuclear weapons certainly posed a threat, the Soviet Union, despite spending three-quarters of its annual revenues on defense, never achieved military parity with the United States, and in 1991, after a mere three years of internal political unrest, it collapsed.

Nevertheless, in 1954, when North Vietnamese communists threatened to overrun the South, the government of the United States sent soldiers to Vietnam and began to conduct military operations against the North. These hostilities, which became known in the United States as the Vietnam War, resulted in the deaths of at least 1,000,000 people.

In the interim, the conflict polarized the American electorate, with half supporting the war and half opposing it. Every year, it seemed, the American public was pummeled by disturbing disclosures about the war, notably the self-immolation of Buddhist monk, Thích Quảng Đức, in the city of Saigon, and the massacre of 347 Vietnamese civilians by American soldiers at Mỹ Lai. Many were surprised to learn that the leader of the North, Ho Chi Minh, had been an American ally during World War Two, and that he fruitlessly had petitioned Presidents Roosevelt and Truman for aid against the French, who previously had colonized Vietnam and brutally oppressed its people.

The disagreement between those who supported and those who opposed the war became so virulent, and persisted for so long, that it can't be explained in terms of differing opinions. Opinions are susceptible to reason and compromise; but world models aren't. Very likely, the vitriolic controversy about the war was fueled by differing world models; the clashing parties simply saw and understood the world differently. Their incendiary rhetoric was fueled by the fear and rage that are evoked whenever the integrity of a world model is threatened by hard facts.

§

A folly is an idea that's widespread but false. For example, many parents refuse to vaccinate their children against known childhood diseases because the vaccines may contain mercury. (Thiomersal, a preservative that at one time was routinely added to vaccines, is a compound of mercury with other elements; mercury is known to interfere with brain development.) Similar reasoning would caution against eating salt because it's a compound of sodium, a corrosive metal, and chlorine, a poisonous gas. The confusion arises from the presumption that an element in a compound has the same chemical properties as the element in its pure form.

A folly can afflict thousands of people over a long period of time. For example, it's generally believed that an airplane manages to stay aloft solely because the morphology of the wings causes moving air to exert more pressure on the lower surface than on the upper. Despite being contradicted by the fact that airplanes are capable of flying upside-down, this explanation is still being taught and is staunchly believed by many to be true.

Like a legal fiction, a folly becomes ensconced as a fact in its adherents' world models and persists because the falsehood that it embodies is believed by a large number of people to be true. Both are dangerous, but a legal fiction is less so because some of its adherents know it to be false; in contrast, those who are ensnared in a folly are cognitively trapped within the worldview that spawned it, and rarely are able to think their way out.

A delusion that's shared by two contending parties is called a folly of two. The two parties need not be individuals; they can be entire populations; and if one or both possess military power, a deadly conflict can ensue.

In 1951, the Iranian parliament took control of Iran's oil industry away from British Petroleum. The British government responded by blockading Iran's seaports. The British offered a settlement, but Iran's Prime Minister, Mohammad Mosaddegh, refused to negotiate with them. The protracted standoff impoverished Iranians, and, in 1953, rather than starving, they removed him from office.

Mosaddegh's downfall also was brought about by his conflicts with political rivals, Shiite clerics, the Iranian military, and the Shah (the king of Iran.)

Nevertheless, it's widely believed by Iranians, and Americans as well, that the sole culprit in the overthrow of Mosaddegh was the government of the United States. But in fact, Great Britain was the main foreign instigator. By comparison, the contribution of the United States was negligible: the Eisenhower administration dispatched Kermit Roosevelt to the Middle East, where his agents did little more than distribute large sums of money to Iranian soldiers and politicians.

Thirty years later, on the pretext of America's putative overthrow of Mosaddegh, Iran's clerical government began the practice of ordering Hezbollah and other proxy militias to kill American soldiers. In 1983, in Beirut, Lebanon, they killed 241 U.S. Marines; in 1985, again in Beirut, they assassinated a U.S. Navy diver; and in 1996, in Khobar, Saudi Arabia, they killed 19 U.S. Airmen.

Imad Fayez Mugniyeh, a Lebanese born resident of Qom, Iran, played a leading role in all three attacks. Mugniyeh was a member of Hezbollah, a Lebanese Shiite militia, and the Islamic Revolutionary Guards Corps (IRGC,) an official branch of the Iranian military.

The religious oligarchy that has ruled Iran since 1979 has continually demonized the United States; taking their cue from them, many Iranians have, for more than forty years, been chanting, "Death to America!" every week during Friday prayers.

§

The advent of the atom bomb in 1945 placed a weapon of unprecedented power into the hands of national leaders who were incapable of understanding it; especially its devastating effects on the human body and its deadly impact on the environment. In 1962, three heads of state — Fidel Castro, Nikita Khrushchev, and John F. Kennedy — brought the world to the brink of nuclear war. In the United States, this incident and the circumstances that precipitated it became known as the Cuban missile crisis.

In order to avoid another nuclear confrontation, nations adopted a policy of sponsoring proxies to do their killing for them. Such behavior is pathological because it makes it easy for a national government to falsely frame the conflict as a religious or ideological struggle, and to needlessly prolong the killing. In contrast, were the war to be prosecuted exclusively by the official armed services of the contending nations, soldiers on both sides would have a strong incentive to minimize the killing and end the war quickly so that they could all go home.

In recent years, sponsors have taken to calling their proxies "freedom fighters," while calling their adversaries' "terrorists." The word, "terrorism," now serves only to confuse the public, which continues to associate it with small, lightly organized, ad hoc amateur insurgent militias. That's what terrorism was in 1970; today, it's a major tool of the foreign policy of several nations.

Proxy wars kill large numbers of people:

- The Korean War (from 1950 to 1953) resulted in the deaths of 3,000,000 people. Initially, it was a war between South Korea and the United States and its allies on one side and North Korea on the other. But it quickly transformed into a war between an American-led coalition on one side and China (the People's Republic of China) on the other, in which South Korea (the Republic of Korea) became a proxy for the United States and North Korea (the Democratic People's Republic of Korea) became a proxy for China.

- The number of people who were killed during the Vietnam War (from 1954 to 1975) is in dispute, with estimates ranging from 1,000,000 to 4,000,000. Initially, it was a conflict between France on one side and Vietnamese communist rebels on the other; but it transformed into a war between the United States and its allies on one side and the Soviet Union and China on the other, in which South Vietnam (the Republic of Vietnam) became a proxy for the United States, and North Vietnam (the Democratic Republic of Vietnam) became a proxy for the Soviet Union and China.

- The Afghan War (from 1979 to 1992) resulted in the deaths of 1,000,000 people. Initially, it was a conflict between the Soviet Union and the Democratic Republic of Afghanistan on one side and a federation of Muslim militias on the other; but it transformed into a war between the Soviet Union on one side and Pakistan and the United States on the other, in which a coalition of Muslim militias was a proxy for Pakistan and the United States.

- The number of people who've been killed during the Kashmir Conflict (from 1947 to the present) is in dispute, with estimates ranging from 40,000 to 90,000. The Kashmir Conflict has been an intermittent war between India and Pakistan (complicated by related hostilities between India and China) in which groups of Muslim insurgents have, from time to time, served as proxies for Pakistan.

- The Second Gulf War (from 2003 to 2011 and from 2013 to 2017) resulted in the deaths of 300,000 people. Initially, it was a war between the United States and its allies on one side and Iraq on the other; but it transformed into a conflict between the American-led coalition on one side and Iran and its proxy insurgent militias on the other.

§

The amok mindset is a cognitive state that enables an aggrieved human male to rationalize murder. A man enters the amok mindset as a result of a repeated, resentful, internal tirade. This diatribe is conducted by his self object and is directed at avatars that represent people who he believes have wronged him. Typically, it's accompanied by feelings of shame and rage. [179]

The monolog is remarkably consistent across cultures, and goes something like this:

> Everything that I ever possessed has been taken from me except my life; a life that now has no value. I feel an intolerable sense of shame and must do something to rehabilitate myself in the eyes of my family. Unlike me, you are favored; but you've achieved your favored state at my expense, through exploitation that's unjust and degrading. If I kill you, then even if I'm killed, the net result will be

> in my favor: my honor will be restored, but yours will
> be taken. But if I cannot kill you, then I will kill either
> members of your family or others like you.

The amok mindset originally was thought to be restricted to Papua, New Guinea; but it regularly occurs in many other countries, including the United States.

Often, a male who's in the process of becoming amok reveals his outrage and desire for revenge to relatives and friends; if he's an adolescent, he may reveal them to a teacher. Such individuals usually are the first to realize that he's becoming a threat. Unfortunately, they rarely intervene, and consequently fail to prevent the killings.

During the past two decades, 20 Americans per year were killed in their workplaces by fellow or former employees. In 1995, a former soldier, assisted by another veteran, bombed the Murrah Federal Office Building in Oklahoma City, Oklahoma, killing 168 people. In 1999, two teenage boys attacked Columbine High School, in Littleton, Colorado, with rifles and homemade bombs, killing a teacher, 12 students, and themselves. And on September 11, 2001, 19 Arab men flew airplanes into the World Trade Center, the Pentagon, and a farmer's field north of Shanksville, Pennsylvania, killing themselves and 2,977 others.

Most of the perpetrators of these attacks were men who'd become amok.

§

An act of evil is an unnecessary killing that's committed for the sake of expediency or entertainment. In his book, "People of the Lie," psychiatrist M. Scott Peck suggests that evil typically is perpetrated by a person who's mendacious, lazy, and narcissistic. [180-181]

The most sensational acts of evil, such as terrorism and genocide, almost invariably are perpetrated by a group of men who are led by a psychopath. Forensic psychologist, Robert Hare, explains in his book, "Without Conscience," that a psychopath feels neither shame nor guilt. [182] Such an individual typically is lazy, mendacious, and narcissistic.

Psychopaths commit 90% of all murders and 50% of all crimes. [183-184]

Psychopathy isn't a psychological dysfunction; it's a neurological pathology. [185] It's usually accompanied by an inability to feel empathy and often diminishes after age forty. [186-187] It isn't caused by childhood abuse and can't be cured through psychotherapy. [188-189]

Psychopaths begin at an early age to victimize others; consequently, their aberrant behavior is susceptible to being detected by parents and teachers before the child is mature enough to cause serious harm. Unfortunately, it's difficult for such mentors to admit to themselves that a youngster who is known to them is a potential criminal; yet it's precisely these people who are best positioned to restrain him.

One psychopath can cause an enormous amount of suffering: Pol Pot, who ordered the killing of 2,000,000 Cambodians, was a psychopath; so was Joseph Stalin, who ordered the assassination of 6,000,000 Soviet citizens; and so was Adolf Hitler, who ordered the liquidation of 6,000,000 Jews.

ξ

Throughout recent history, large numbers of people have needlessly been slain. Among the many and disparate causes of these killings, hidden in plain sight, has been a surprisingly short list of pathological behaviors: legal fictions, follies of two, war by proxy, the amok mindset, and psychopathy:

- Throughout the Cold War, Americans believed that a putative Soviet-led conspiracy called "world communism" posed a mortal danger to the United States. On the basis of this legal fiction, the American government attacked Vietnam and thereby caused the deaths of between 1,000,000 and 4,000,000 people.

- When, in 1953, the government of the Iranian Prime Minister, Mohammad Mosaddegh, was overthrown, both Iranians and Americans believed that the coup had been instigated exclusively by the United States. By virtue of this folly of two, the American government became leery of opposing Iran, and the Iranian government began to kill Americans in large numbers.

- Over the past 73 years, there have been five major proxy wars: the Korean War, the Vietnam War, the Afghan War, the Kashmir

Conflict, and the Second Gulf War. All told, these hostilities have resulted in the deaths of more than 5,000,000 people.

- In the 2001 attack by Muslim extremists upon New York City and Washington, D.C., 17 of the perpetrators were men who had adopted the amok mindset; altogether, they killed nearly 3,000 people.

- In the first half of the twentieth century, two psychopaths became heads of state: Joseph Stalin in the Soviet Union and Adolph Hitler in Germany. Stalin ordered the assassination of 6,000,000 of his own people, and Hitler ordered the execution of 6,000,000 Jews.

It isn't hard to imagine that, in the brains of the right individuals, under the right circumstances, such pathological behaviors could precipitate Armageddon.

Chapter 22: Selective Brutalization

In mammalian species that are highly social, adolescent males fight and jostle with their peers for status and dominance. In the process, they learn to be tough, to ignore pain, and to suppress fear; [190] the purpose of this transformation is to enable them to defend their families against aggression by others. This process, which is called brutalization, is overseen by mature males who are members of their primary groups. (An animal's primary group is a circle of intimates that includes the animal, itself, and its closest relatives and friends.) [191]

In a family, an ongoing balance must be maintained between brutality and empathy. Empathy is the ability to imagine the pain and suffering of another. Without empathy, males might kill other family members; but without brutality, they'd be unable to defend them. The web of social rules that binds the family together prescribes limits on intrafamilial violence but permits unconstrained aggression against outsiders; yet even in this case, innate neurological processes limit the killing.

For instance, during the Civil War, at the Battle of Gettysburg, only 10% of the men of both sides fired their weapons; during World War Two, only 20% of U.S. soldiers fired theirs; but during the Vietnam War, 90% of American combatants fired their weapons at the Vietnamese. [192]

What had changed that so dramatically had increased the brutality of American soldiers? [193]

The practice of brutalization is ethical if it's applied uniformly to all young men and if its aim is to defend the family. Unfortunately, it's possible to brutalize boys for purposes that have nothing to do with protecting their kinfolk. [194] If they are isolated from their extended families and kept under the thumb of a victimizer, they can be imbued with excessive brutality. Ideal environments for this kind of mistreatment are prisons, gangs, isolated private schools, abusive nuclear families, and boot camps (military camps where soldiers undergo basic training.) [195-197] Because it isn't practiced uniformly on all young men, such abuse is called selective brutalization.

The process of selective brutalization has three components: subjugation, horrification, and violent coaching; [198] this nomenclature was developed by criminologist, Lonnie Athens, and is explained in Richard Rhodes's book, "Why They Kill." Each component is a campaign of social transactions between three protagonists: the coach, who directs the process; the novice, who is to be brutalized, and is, himself, a victim; and a third participant who functions as a victim or a witness.

Subjugation is the infliction of violence by the coach upon the novice. [199] Horrification is the witnessing, by the novice, of violence being inflicted by the coach upon a third participant. [200] Violent coaching is instruction by the coach with the aim of causing the novice to inflict violence upon a third party. [201] All three campaigns are augmented by ridicule, haranguing, coercing, and besiegement. [202-206] The novice is incessantly assailed via these devices and eventually gives up all efforts to resist.

What subjugation, horrification, and violent coaching have in common is that they induce shame within the novice: subjugation produces shame because the novice has not had the power, courage, or determination to fight back; horrification produces shame because he has stood by and done nothing to defend the victim; and violent coaching produces shame because he needlessly has harmed, or someday may harm, another person.

Shame is an adaptation that's designed to ensure that a male fulfills his responsibility to defend the family. By commandeering this powerful neurological machinery, selective brutalization suppresses empathy, unleashes brutality, and transforms the novice from a defender of the family into a defender of the coach's constituency; the constituency then directs the novice's brutality against an adversary or scapegoat that it previously has selected. [207]

Boot camp drill instructors routinely brutalize their recruits. Men who comply quickly are spared most of the punishment; the abuse chiefly is directed against those who either are incompetent or have sufficient backbone to refuse to obey the instructor. Once such a recruit has been identified, the process goes into overdrive and mercilessly grinds him down.

Neurologically, the drama of selective brutalization takes place primarily within the family shell of cognition between the autobiographical self and avatars that represent the other parties. (Boot camp drill instructors, in effect, forcibly insert the other protagonists into the recruits' primary groups.) But selective brutalization can be conducted much more thoroughly, albeit more slowly, in the imaging shell.

The mission of the imaging shell is to objectify complex visual images, including sensational depictions of war, murder, and personal combat. This renders the extended self vulnerable to vicarious brutalization through motion pictures and television. [208] In the United States, the proportion of households that had televisions increased from 9% in 1950 to 95% in 1969; [209] approximately 2,000,000 American boys who grew up during this period were drafted, during the late 1960s, to fight in Vietnam.

Very likely, the increase in the proportion of American soldiers who fired at the enemy, which reached 90% during the Vietnam War, [210] was due to their unprecedented exposure to televised subjugation, horrification, and violent coaching throughout their childhoods. [211] Tragically, when they came home, except for those who had the good fortune to be welcomed by a competent extended family, none of them were processed through an inverse boot camp that could unwind their brutality and reinstate their empathy. Thousands became walking time bombs, ready to explode whenever misfortune chose to visit them again. [212]

Chapter 23: The Shrinking Primary Group

Every member of a social mammalian species has a circle of intimates called a primary group. The animal, itself, is a member of its own primary group; so is its mother, at least initially, and sometimes for a lifetime; and so are its closest relatives and friends. The primary group, by virtue of its collective life experience, is the animal's main source of knowledge. [213] The number of members in an individual's intimate circle is a homeostatic parameter, the maximal acceptable value of which varies by species; but for all species, the minimal acceptable value is two.

The shrinking primary group is a pattern of social impoverishment that's characterized by a persistent decline in the number of members in an animal's primary group. Within such an individual's brain, this diminution reduces the self object's main source of information and produces an intolerable feeling of anxiety. The purpose of this anxiety is to impel the animal to recruit, as quickly as possible, new members into its primary group. So powerful is this drive that if the primary group collapses altogether, rather than living alone, the animal will bond with some other animal, not necessarily of the same species.

The brain is an exquisitely crafted organ; a biological mechanism that's continuously been refined over 650 million years. It's astonishingly robust and resilient; but, like any other machine, it has weaknesses that, under particular circumstances, can cause it to fail. One of its most vulnerable parts is the family shell of cognition. An individual animal has little control over the survival resources that are provided by its extended family; if the amount of such a resource is too high or too low, the animal can't function properly. In effect, such quantities are homeostatic parameters.

For a social animal, one of its most important homeostatic parameters is the number of members in its extended family. The optimal value of this number varies by species, but for humans, it's 150 or thereabouts. [214] However, in the modern industrial west, people live in nuclear families and rarely interact with many of their other relatives; consequently, their primary groups are either too small [215] or too infrequently available to provide them with intimate, ongoing, and effective counsel. This insufficient guidance is particularly detrimental to adolescent boys, especially if their fathers are dead, absent, or otherwise unavailable. [216-217]

A boy can compensate for an inadequate primary group by bonding with boys of other families. Such a gang exerts a profound influence over him that easily can escape his family's notice; for it operates not only when he's with the gang, but also when he's alone. Within his brain, his self object converses frequently with avatars that represent the other gang members. This ongoing internal dialog greatly influences him because it can't be turned off.

Although a cobbled-together primary group is no substitute for the real thing, at the least, it enables a boy to become a productive member of society. However, because middle-class families often move away whenever their breadwinners get new jobs, an ad hoc primary group is susceptible to shrinking. Deaths, illnesses, and arguments among its members also can cause a primary group to shrink. Thus, by a combination of bad luck and poor choices, the population of such a group can decline until it reaches its lowest possible value: two. Such a duo is called a binary gang.

If a boy becomes a member of a binary gang, within his brain, the ongoing internal discussion that's normally conducted between his self object and avatars that represent his family can become supplanted by a one-on-one conversation between his self object and the avatar that represents his partner. Under these circumstances, the partner's life experience can become the boy's primary source of knowledge, and the partner's values can supplant those of the boy's family, especially if the partner is dominant and the other boy is submissive.

If a binary gang begins to engage in criminal activity, it can become a mortal danger. Two physically mature males, one or both of whom are criminals, and who are closely bound to each other, can do much more harm together than one man can do alone. For instance, by working together, Timothy McVeigh and Terry Nichols were able to load more than 5,000 pounds of ammonium nitrate and nitromethane into the cargo bay of their Ryder truck.

[218] Nichols also assisted McVeigh in stealing 500 electric blasting caps and 80 spools of shock cord from a quarry in Marion, Kansas. If McVeigh had attempted to do all this alone, his intention to construct a bomb almost certainly would have been detected.

McVeigh's collaboration with Nichols resulted in the deaths of 168 people. An analysis of his biography strongly suggests that the main cause of the Oklahoma City bombing was the catastrophic collapse of Timothy McVeigh's primary group.

A brain that's been deprived of an adequate primary group is as predictably dysfunctional as a brain that's been deprived of an adequate supply of glucose. In both cases, the brain is pushed beyond its homeostatic limits. The fact that many boys manage to survive such deficiencies simply means that the brain, because of its robustness and resiliency, often finds a way to compensate for what's missing; but such makeshift measures can't be sustained indefinitely.

Chapter 24: Juvenile Domestic Terrorism

Topographic psychology can help to explain one of the most puzzling features of contemporary life: juvenile domestic terrorism; an act of murder in which two young men kill multiple people indiscriminately:

1. On April 19, 1995, a decorated veteran of the First Gulf War, supported by another former soldier, detonated a truck bomb in front of the Alfred Murrah Federal Office Building in Oklahoma City, Oklahoma. The blast destroyed the structure and killed 168 people.

2. On April 20, 1999, two teenage boys attacked Columbine High School, in Littleton, Colorado, with rifles and homemade bombs. During a 46-minute rampage, they killed a teacher and 12 students, wounded 24 others, and then shot themselves.

3. On January 27, 2001, two teenage boys slashed the throats of two wealthy, well-known scholars, who were professors at nearby Dartmouth College in Hanover, New Hampshire.

4. On October 2, 2002, and over a period of 20 days thereafter, two men, one of them in his teens, shot 13 people, killing 10 of them, in locations that roughly formed an arc around Washington, D.C., along the Capital Beltway.

None of these killings was done to protect the killers, or their families, from aggression by others; nor to bind together the family or raise children; nor to obtain food, shelter, or territory. In the Columbine High School massacre and the Dartmouth College murders, one of the perpetrators was a psychopath; and in the Oklahoma City bombing and the Columbine High School massacre, one of the perpetrators was amok.

The protagonist of an act of juvenile domestic terrorism typically is a young male who's a member of a dysfunctional, incohesive, or dissolved nuclear family. Because his parents and siblings are preoccupied with coping with the family's problems, they fail to notice subtle but significant changes in his behavior. As he approaches his twentieth birthday, or thereabouts, he fails to obtain or hold onto gainful employment, and fails to establish a stable relationship with a woman; instead, he careens from job to job and from girlfriend to girlfriend.

Out of frustration or desperation, he commits a crime; but none of the family's other members seem to notice. Having failed to gain their attention, he follows up by committing a series of increasingly dangerous offenses. Simultaneously, through bad luck, changing circumstances, or petty frictions, his social and familial relationships begin to disappear.

As the population of his primary group decreases, the only meaningful relationship that endures is his fellowship with his best friend; in many cases, a boy of his own age with whom he's been close friends since childhood. They become a tightly bound binary gang in which he is the dominant member. He then entices his partner into joining him in his criminal activities. Finally, having despaired of ever holding a good job, or of siring and supporting legitimate children, he adopts the amok mindset and selects the scapegoats who shortly will become his victims. His companion submissively follows his lead.

By the time he was 14 years of age, the chief perpetrator of the Oklahoma City Bombing, Timothy McVeigh, had suffered three blows to his head. Such injuries are thought to place a boy at risk for committing violent crimes as an adult.

This notwithstanding, the root cause of the Oklahoma City Bombing was the catastrophic collapse of Timothy McVeigh's primary group: Had McVeigh been able to hang on to the caring extended family into which he'd been born; had he been able to keep his many high school friends; had his parents not divorced; had his mother and sisters not moved far away; had his father remained present and active in his life; had his commander cared enough to dissuade him from quitting the Army, where he'd been highly valued for his marksmanship and leadership; and had his paternal grandfather, Ed, with whom he had bonded closely, not died suddenly, McVeigh might never have killed 168 innocent people in Oklahoma City.

In hunter-gatherer societies, where such crimes never occur, only the death of a close relative is unavoidable; analogs of McVeigh's other losses rarely happen. But in the modern west, where juvenile domestic terrorism is endemic, such losses are common and seem unremarkable. Under these circumstances, it's difficult to identify a burgeoning domestic terrorist. However, two physically mature boys who are so tightly bound together that they rarely interact with anyone else are highly visible.

Chapter 25: Summary and Conclusion

Although today, as in Freud's day, many people are suffering with private, emotional issues, all of us, together, are facing unprecedented threats that are large, complex, intractable, and deadly, the most serious of which are climate change and the proliferation of nuclear weapons. But the rapid growth, over the past three decades, in our understanding of the brain has presented us with an opportunity to explain both adaptive and pathological behaviors in neurological terms. If our problems, large and small, can be traced to the ordinary operations of the brain, remedies that previously had been invisible may be uncovered.

Topographic psychology provides a set of concepts that can serve this purpose. All of them already have been explored in the literatures of science and psychology; but none heretofore have been recognized as being general or fundamental. In this concluding chapter, it's appropriate to briefly review them.

§

All life-forms transform sensation into motion, systematically obtain raw materials from the environment, construct a self, procreate, and cycle continually between eating, avoiding being eaten, and reproducing; [219] of these behaviors, the transformation of sensation into motion is the most fundamental and is the bedrock upon which the other four were constructed.

The fossil record suggests that all extant life-forms descended from a bacterium-like species that lived 3.5 billion years ago; [220] all of their behaviors evolved from the activities of this common ancestor.

In order to understand behavior, it's useful to conceive of the brain as a biological machine that utilizes a subjective internal world model to transform sensation into motion. This conception renders superfluous the concept of the mind. One instance of transforming sensation into motion is called a decision odyssey; a decision odyssey is a virtual voyage that originates as sensation, passes through the body, and emerges as motion; within the context of this paradigm, a decision is whatever cognition takes place along the route via which the odyssey passes through the body.

The brain of a vertebrate is composed of a sequence of five neural shells that are nested, one within another, like the hollow wooden figures in a set of Russian Dolls. [221] Inhabiting the brain's central axis is an artifact called the self object, whose purpose is to represent internally the body of the owner of the brain; because the self object participates in all decisions, it necessarily intersects with each of the neural shells, and, consequently, is likewise composed of five nested parts.

The self object is an outgrowth of a converging network of nerves that originate in sensory arrays throughout the body; they convey to the brain a composite representation of the state of the whole organism; this composite image is the foundation of the internal sense of self.

In general, an animal interacts with only one other animal at a time; whenever it does so, the other party usually reciprocates; such an event pair is called a binary transaction, and each event is called a unitary action. What an animal does in these interactions largely is determined by the contents of its world model, by its internal autobiography, and by the current physiological state of its body; there are three such states: violence, sex, and work. [222] A unitary action is executed by a dispositional representation called an effector. An effector binds together neural artifacts that represent the owner of the brain, the other party, and the action that one participant performs upon the other.

Conducting internal dialogs, telling stories to oneself, and assembling chains of reasoning are principal forms of thinking. Thinking utilizes three kinds of neural artifacts: objects, connections, and transactions. In hominins, the evolutionary antecedents of rational thinking were sequencing, analogizing, and tracking. The main benefit of language is that it dramatically speeds up thinking.

The brain is, in many ways, like a computer or a network of computers:

1. The social complexity of a family is like the connective complexity of the Internet.

2. Interactions between family members are like transactions between Internet computers.

3. The neural shells of the vertebrate brain are similar to the communications layers of the Internet.

4. A dispositional representation in the brain is like a software program in a computer.

5. The digest of an image in the brain is like the digest of a sequence of data in a computer.

6. Vertebrate color vision is similar to computer color graphics.

7. Vertebrate nighttime vision is similar to computer grayscale graphics.

8. The representation in the brain of a visual referent is similar to the representation in a computer of a three-dimensional figure.

9. A story or a chain of inference in the brain is similar to a linked list of records in a database.

10. A neuron in the brain that possesses an autapse is like a timer chip in a computer.

11. Accessing an internalized referent by name is like retrieving a computer record by hashing.

12. The swapping of bodily contexts by the brain is like the swapping of operational modes by a finite state machine.

13. Multitasking in the brain is like parallel processing in a vector or array processor.

Human behavior is orchestrated by hundreds of nuclei that reside in the brain, including the thalamus, the hypothalamus, the pituitary, the superior colliculus, the hippocampus, the amygdala, and the locus coeruleus. Nuclei, glands, and organs in total secrete as many as 200 kinds of molecular messengers, including oxytocin, vasopressin, melanocyte-stimulating hormone, thyroid-stimulating hormone, follicle-stimulating hormone, growth hormone, adrenocoricotropic hormone, prolactin, dopamine, serotonin, histamine, glutamate, acetylcholine, and norepinephrine.

Not all homeostatic limits apply to processes inside the body; some pertain to social interactions that take place outside. Among these external parameters are the number of members in an individual's extended family and the number of members in its primary group. If the values of these parameters are too small, severe problems can ensue.

The optimal number of members in an extended family of humans is 150.

Deadly societal dysfunctions, such as murder, genocide, terrorism, and war, can be precipitated by a relatively small set of pathological behaviors: legal fictions, follies of two, war by proxy, the amok mindset, and psychopathy.

Murder is committed mainly by men who are amok or psychopathic.

In general, the chief perpetrators of an act of foreign terrorism are amok men who are led by a psychopath. Typically, the chief perpetrator of an act of juvenile domestic terrorism is a relatively young man whose primary group has suffered a catastrophic collapse.

§

Topographic psychology predicts that any credible study of criminal statistics that have been gathered from a set of randomly selected communities will reveal the following:

1. On the average, the number of crimes per household is inversely related to the number of adult occupants per household.

2. In serious crimes, the most frequent number of perpetrators is two.

§

Compelling evidence suggests that we were designed by Nature to regularly walk, and periodically run, great distances; to eat many kinds of plants supplemented by cooked meat; to live in small communities in which everyone knows everyone else; and, at all times, to be attentive to matters of survival. [223-226]

All of our ancestors succeeded in living long enough to bear children and raise them to child bearing age; only during the most recent 12,000 years did any of our forebears depend on agriculture, industry, technology, organized religion, government, or laws. The rules of right living were imposed upon them by their daily struggle to survive, the necessity of protecting everyone, [227] the example of their elders, and the quiet voices of their genes.

Although a wholesale refashioning of the western way of life is impractical, there's nothing to prevent a sufficiently motivated family from quietly seceding in place from western society and beginning to live as Nature intended. No doubt, there would be challenges to their survival. Life is unpredictable and inherently dangerous. But, somehow, the goodness of life and the dangers that beset it go together; one would be meaningless without the other.

Bibliography

1. Albus, James S., The Engineering of Mind (Intelligent Systems Division, National Institute of Standards and Technology, Gaithersburg, MD)

2. "Annual_TV_Households_50-78.JPG," the TV History Website, http://www.tvhistory.tv/facts-stats.htm

3. Ardrey, Robert, The Territorial Imperative: A Personal Inquiry into the Animal Origins of Property and Nations (New York, 1966: Atheneum)

4. Aristotle, Politics.

5. Atkins, P. W. and Beran, J. A., General Chemistry, Second Edition (New York, 1992: Scientific American Library)

6. "avatar," Microsoft Encarta Dictionary (1999)

7. "avatar," Webster's Encyclopedic Unabridged Dictionary of the English Language (1989)

8. Baggott, Jim, Origins: The Scientific Story of Creation (New York, 2015: Oxford University Press)

9. Barash, David P., The Survival Game: How Game Theory Explains the Biology of Cooperation and Competition (New York, 2003: Times Books - Henry Holt and Company)

10. Bejan, Adrian and Zane, J. Peder, Design in Nature: How the Constructal Law Governs Evolution in Biology, Physics, Technology, and Social Organization (New York, 2012: Random House-Doubleday)

11. Berman, Bob, "Body of Work", Discover, July/August 2014

Bibliography

12.   Berne, Eric, Games People Play: The Basic Handbook of Transactional Analysis (New York, 1964: Ballantine Books)

13.   Blum, Deborah, Love at Goon Park: Harry Harlow and the Science of Affection (Cambridge, Massachusetts, 2002: Perseus Publishing)

14.   Bly, Robert, Iron John: A Book About Men (New York, 1990: Random House - Vintage)

15.   Bly, Robert, The Sibling Society (New York, 1996: Addison-Wesley Publishing Company)

16.   Boeree, C. George, "Abraham Maslow" (Department of Psychology, Shippensburg University of Pennsylvania, 1998: http:// www.ship. edu/~cgboeree/ maslow.html)

17.   Boesch, Christophe, "Complex Cooperation among Taï Chimpanzees" in de Waal, Frans B. M. and Tyack, Peter L., editors, Animal Social Complexity: Intelligence, Culture, and Individualized Societies (Cambridge, Massachusetts, 2003: Harvard University Press)

18.   Brodal, Per, The Central Nervous System: Structure and Function, Third Edition (New York, 2004: Oxford University Press)

19.   Brown, Dee, Bury My Heart at Wounded Knee: An Indian History of the American West (New York, 2000: Henry Holt and Company - Owl Books)

20.   Brown, Guy, The Energy of Life: The Science of What Makes our Minds and Bodies Work (New York, 2000: Simon and Schuster - The Free Press)

21.   Calaprice, Alice, editor, The Expanded Quotable Einstein (Princeton, New Jersey, 2000: Princeton University Press)

22.   Carter, Rita, Mapping the Mind (Los Angeles, California, 1998: University of California Press)

23.   Cavalieri, Paola and Singer, Peter, editors, The Great Ape Project: Equality Beyond Humanity (New York, 1993: St. Martin's - Griffin)

24. Chamovitz, Daniel, What a Plant Knows: A Field Guide to the Senses (New York, 2012: Scientific American/Farrar, Straus and Giroux)

25. Churchland, Patricia Smith, Neurophilosophy: Toward a Unified Science of Mind- Brain (Cambridge, Massachusetts, 1988: The MIT Press - Bradford Books)

26. Churchland, Paul M., A Neurocomputational Perspective: The Nature of Mind and the Structure of Science (Cambridge, Massachusetts, 2000: The MIT Press - Bradford Books)

27. Churchland, Paul M., The Engine of Reason, the Seat of the Soul: A Philosophical Journey into the Brain (Cambridge, Massachusetts, 1996: The MIT Press - Bradford Books)

28. Clark, Stephen R. L., "Apes and the Idea of Kindred" in Cavalieri, Paola and Singer, Peter, editors, The Great Ape Project: Equality Beyond Humanity (New York, 1993: St. Martin's - Griffin)

29. Comer, Douglas E., Internetworking With TCP/IP: Principles, Protocols, and Architecture (Englewood Cliffs, New Jersey, 1988: Simon and Schuster - Prentice-Hall)

30. Conway, Martin A., Cognitive Models of Memory (Cambridge, Massachusetts, 1997: The MIT Press)

31. Cropper, William H., Great Physicists: The Life and Times of Leading Physicists from Galileo to Hawking (New York, 2001: Oxford University Press)

32. Damasio, Antonio and Damasio, Hanna, "Making Images and Creating Subjectivity" in Llinás, Rodolfo R. and Churchland, Patricia S., The Mind-Brain Continuum: Sensory Processes (Cambridge, Massachusetts, 1998: The MIT Press - Bradford Books)

33. Damasio, Antonio, Descartes' Error: Emotion, Reason and the Human Brain (New York, 2000: Harper-Collins - Quill)

34. Damasio, Antonio, Looking for Spinoza: Joy, Sorrow and the Feeling Brain (New York, 2003: Harcourt)

35.   Damasio, Antonio, Self Comes to Mind: Constructing the Conscious Brain (New York, 2010: Pantheon Books)

36.   Damasio, Antonio, The Feeling of What Happens: Body and Emotion in the Making of Consciousness (New York, 1999: Harcourt - Harvest)

37.   Darwin, Charles, The Origin of Species by Means of Natural Selection or Preservation of Favoured Races in the Struggle for Life (New York, 1985: New American Library)

38.   Davenport, David, From Mind to Brain Machine: The Architecture of Cognition (Bilkent University, Department of Computer Engineering, Ankara, Turkey), 2000.

39.   Dawkins, Richard, The Ancestor's Tale: A Pilgrimage to the Dawn of Evolution (New York, 2004: Houghton Mifflin)

40.   Dawkins, Richard, The Selfish Gene (New York, 1999: Oxford University Press)

41.   de Duve, Christian, Life Evolving: Molecules, Mind, and Meaning (New York, 2002: Oxford University Press)

42.   de Waal, Frans B. M. and Aureli, Filippo, "Conflict Resolution and Distress Alleviation in Monkeys and Apes" in Carter, C. Sue, Lederhendler, Izja, and Kilpatrick, Brian, editors, The Integrative Neurobiology of Affiliation (Cambridge, Massachusetts, 1999: The MIT Press - Bradford Books)

43.   de Waal, Frans B. M. and Tyack, Peter L., editors, Animal Social Complexity: Intelligence, Culture, and Individualized Societies (Cambridge, Massachusetts, 2003: Harvard University Press)

44.   de Waal, Frans B. M., The Ape and the Sushi Master: Cultural Reflections of a Primatologist (New York, 2001: Perseus - Basic Books)

45.   Dehaene, Stanislas, Consciousness and the Brain: Deciphering How the Brain Codes our Thoughts (New York, 2014: Penguin)

46.   Dehaene, Stanislas, Reading in the Brain: The Science and Evolution of a Human Invention (New York, 2009: Viking - Penguin)

47.   Diamond, Jared, Guns, Germs, and Steel: The Fates of Human Societies (New York, 1999: W. W. Norton and Company)

48.   Diamond, Jared, The World Until Yesterday: What Can We Learn from Traditional Societies? (New York, 2012: Penguin Books)

49.   Dixson, Danielle L., "Lost at Sea", Scientific American, June 2017

50.   Dulbecco, Renato, The Design of Life (New Haven, Connecticut, 1987: Yale University Press)

51.   Dunbar, Robin and Barrett, Louise, Cousins: Our Primate Relatives (London, 2000: BBC Worldwide Limited)

52.   Dunbar, Robin, "Brains on Two Legs", in de Waal, Frans B. M. and Tyack, Peter L., editors, Animal Social Complexity: Intelligence, Culture, and Individualized Societies (Cambridge, Massachusetts, 2003: Harvard University Press)

53.   Dunbar, Robin, "Brains on Two Legs: Group Size and the Evolution of Intelligence" in de Waal, Frans B. M., editor, Tree of Origin: What Primate Behavior Can Tell Us about Human Social Evolution (Cambridge, Massachusetts, 2002: Harvard University Press)

54.   Eccles, John C., Evolution of the Brain: Creation of the Self (London, UK, 1989: Routledge)

55.   Ellsberg, Daniel, Secrets: A Memoir of Vietnam and the Pentagon Papers (New York, 2002: Viking -Penguin)

56.   Faludi, Susan, Stiffed: The Betrayal of the American Man (New York, 1999: William Morrow and Company, Inc.)

57.   Fields, R. Douglas, The Other Brain: From Dementia to Schizophrenia, How New Discoveries about the Brain Are Revolutionizing Medicine and Science (New York, 2009: Simon and Schuster)

58.   Fouts, Roger S. and Fouts, Deborah H., "Chimpanzees' Use of Sign Language", in Cavalieri, Paola and Singer, Peter, editors, The Great Ape Project: Equality Beyond Humanity (New York, 1993: St. Martin's - Griffin)

59.   Fouts, Roger, and Mills, Stephen Tukel, Next of Kin: My Conversations with Chimpanzees (New York, 1997: Avon Books)

60.   Freud, Sigmund, Beyond the Pleasure Principle, 1920.

61.   Gärdenfors, Peter, Conceptual Spaces: The Geometry of Thought (Cambridge, Massachusetts, 2000: The MIT Press - Bradford Books)

62.   Gazzaniga, Michael S., Ivry, Richard B., and Mangun, George R., Cognitive Neuroscience: The Biology of the Mind, Second Edition (New York, 2002: W. W. Norton)

63.   Gellatly, Angus and Zarate, Oscar, Introducing Mind and Brain (Cambridge, UK, 1999: Icon Books, Limited)

64.   Ghiglieri, Michael P., The Dark Side of Man: Tracing the Origins of Male Violence (Cambridge, Massachusetts, 1999: Perseus - Helix)

65.   Gluck, Mark A. and Myers, Catherine E., Gateway to Memory: An Introduction to Neural Network Modeling of the Hippocampus and Learning (Cambridge, Massachusetts, 2001: MIT Press - Bradford Books)

66.   Glynn, Ian, An Anatomy of Thought: The Origin and Machinery of the Mind (New York, 1999: Oxford University Press)

67.   Goodale, Melvyn A. and Humphrey, G. Keith, "The Objects of Action and Perception", in Tarr, Michael J. and Bülthoff, Heinrich H., Object Recognition in Man, Monkey, and Machine (Boston, Massachusetts, 1998: The MIT Press)

68.   Goodall, Jane, In the Shadow of Man, Revised edition (New York, 2000: Houghton Mifflin - Mariner)

69.	Goodall, Jane, Through a Window: My 30 Years with the Chimpanzees of Gombe (New York, 1990: Houghton Miflin - Mariner)

70.	Gould, Edwin and McKay, George, editors, Encyclopedia of Mammals: A Comprehensive Illustrated Guide by International Experts, Second edition (San Francisco, California, 1998: Fog City Press)

71.	Graham, Alistair and Beard, Peter, Eyelids of Morning: The Mingled Destinies of Crocodiles and Men (San Francisco, California, 1990: Chronicle Books)

72.	Grandin, Temple, with Johnson, Catherine, Animals in Translation: Using the Mysteries of Autism to Decode Animal Behavior (New York, 2005: Scribner)

73.	Greene, Brian, The Elegant Universe: Superstrings, Hidden Dimensions, and the Quest for the Ultimate Theory (New York, 1999: Vintage Books)

74.	Griffin, Donald R., The Question of Animal Awareness: Evolutionary Continuity of Mental Experience (New York, 1976: The Rockefeller University Press)

75.	Griggs, Mary Beth, "Dead or Alive: What's the Meaning of Life?" Popular Science, Summer 2018, page 10.

76.	Grossman, David, On Killing: The Psychological Costs of Learning to Kill in War and Society (Boston, Massachusetts, 1996: Little, Brown and Company - Back Bay Books)

77.	Harari, Yuval Noah, Sapiens: A Brief History of Humankind (New York, 2015: HarperCollins)

78.	Hare, Robert D., Without Conscience: The Disturbing World of the Psychopaths Among Us (New York, 1999: The Guilford Press)

79.	Harnish, Robert M., Minds, Brains, Computers: An Historical Introduction to the Foundations of Cognitive Science (Oxford, UK: 2002, Blackwell Publishers, Inc.)

80. Hawkins, Jeff, and Blakeslee, Sandra, On Intelligence: How a New Understanding of the Brain Will Lead to the Creation of Truly Intelligent Machines (New York, 2004: Times Books - Henry Holt)

81. Hoffman, Peter M., Life's Ratchet: How Molecular Machines Extract Order from Chaos (New York, 2012: Perseus Books Group - Basic Books)

82. Hofstadter, Douglas R. and Sander, Emmanuel, Surfaces and Essences: Analogy as the Fuel and Fire of Thinking (New York, 2013: Perseus - Basic)

83. Hofstadter, Douglas R., Gödel, Escher, Bach: An Eternal Golden Braid: A Metaphorical Fugue on Minds and Machines in the Spirit of Lewis Carroll (New York, 1979: Random House - Vintage)

84. Horwitz, Joshua, War of the Whales: A True Story (New York, 2014: Simon and Schuster)

85. Ishida, Jintaro, The Remains of War: Apology and Forgiveness (Guilford, Connecticut, 2002: Lyons Press)

86. Johanson, Donald and Edey, Maitland, Lucy: The Beginnings of Humankind (New York, 1981: Simon and Schuster - Touchstone)

87. Johnson, Steven, "The Brain and Emotions: Fear", Discover, March 2003, page 36.

88. Katz, Jonathan I., The Biggest Bangs: The Mystery of Gamma-ray Bursts, the Most Violent Explosions in the Universe (New York, 2002: Oxford University Press)

89. Keen, Sam, Fire in the Belly: On Being a Man (New York, 1991: Bantam Books)

90. Keenan, Julian Paul, Gallup, Gordon G., and Falk, Dean, The Face in the Mirror: The Search for the Origins of Consciousness (New York, 2003: HarperCollins Publishers, Inc.)

91. Keijzer, Fred, Representation and Behavior (Cambridge, Massachusetts, 2001: The MIT Press - Bradford Books)

92. Kilmartin, Christopher T., The Masculine Self, Second edition (New York, 2000: McGraw-Hill)

93. Koch, Christof, The Quest for Consciousness: A Neurobiological Approach (Englewood, Colorado, 2004: Roberts and Company, Publishers)

94. Kortlandt, Adriaan, "Spirits Dressed in Furs?", in Cavalieri, Paola and Singer, Peter, editors, The Great Ape Project: Equality Beyond Humanity (New York, 1993: St. Martin's - Griffin)

95. Kramer, Robert, Beyond Max Weber: Emotional Intelligence and Public Leadership (School of Public Affairs, American University, Washington, D.C.)

96. Kruuk, Hans, Niko's Nature: A life of Niko Tinbergen and his science of animal behavior (Oxford, UK, 2003: Oxford University Press)

97. Kurzweil, Ray, How to Create a Mind: The Secret of Human Thought Revealed (New York, 2012: Viking - Penguin)

98. Lane, Nick, The Vital Question: Energy, Evolution, and the Origins of Complex Life (New York, 2015: W. W. Norton & Company Ltd.)

99. LeDoux, Joseph, Synaptic Self: How Our Brains Become Who We Are (New York, 2002: Viking - Penguin)

100. Livingstone, Margaret, Vision and Art: The Biology of Seeing (New York, 2002: Harry. N. Abrams, Inc.)

101. Llinás, Rodolfo R. and Paré, D., "The Brain as a Closed System Modulated by the Senses", in Llinás, Rodolfo R. and Churchland, Patricia S., The Mind-Brain Continuum: Sensory Processes (Cambridge, Massachusetts, 1998: The MIT Press - Bradford Books)

102. Llinás, Rodolfo R., i of the vortex: From Neurons to Self (Cambridge, Massachusetts, 2002: The MIT Press - Bradford Books)

103. Lopez, Barry Holstun, Of Wolves and Men (New York, 1978: Charles Scribner's Sons)

Bibliography

104. Lorenz, Konrad, On Aggression (New York, 1966: MJF Books)

105. Lorenz, Konrad, The Natural Science of the Human Species: An Introduction to Comparative Behavioral Research: The "Russian Manuscript" (1944 - 1948) (Cambridge, Massachusetts, 1997: The MIT Press)

106. Lynch, Gary and Baudry, Michel, "Structure-Function Relationships in the Organization of Memory" in Gazzaniga, Michael S., Ivry, Richard B., and Mangun, George R., Cognitive Neuroscience: The Biology of the Mind, Second Edition (New York, 2002: W. W. Norton)

107. MacLean, Paul D., The Triune Brain in Evolution: Role in Paleocerebral Functions (New York, 1990: Plenum Publishing)

108. Macknik, Stephen L. and Martinez-Conde, Susana, "What a Trip: Take a visual journey through seven prizewinning illusions", Scientific American Mind, May/June 2014, pages 66-67.

109. Mallot, Hanspeter A., translated by Allen, John S., Computational Vision: Information Processing in Perception and Visual Behavior (Cambridge, Massachusetts, 2000: The MIT Press - Bradford Books)

110. Malsburg, C. von der, "The Binding Problem of Neural Networks" in Llinás, Rodolfo R. and Churchland, Patricia S., The Mind-Brain Continuum: Sensory Processes (Cambridge, Massachusetts, 1998: The MIT Press - Bradford Books)

111. Margulis, Lynn and Sagan, Dorion, Microcosms: Four Billion Years of Microbial Evolution (Berkley and Los Angeles, California, 1986: University of California Press)

112. Margulis, Lynn and Sagan, Dorion, What is Life? (Berkley and Los Angeles, California, 1995: University of California Press)

113. Margulis, Lynn, Symbiotic Planet: A New Look at Evolution (New York, 1998: Perseus Books Group - Basic Books)

114. Maslow, Abraham, Motivation and Personality, 1954.

115. Mayer, Emeran, The Mind-Gut Connection: How the Hidden Conversation Within Our Bodies Impacts Our Mood, Our Choices, and Our Overall Health (New York, 2016: HarperCollins)

116. Mayr, Ernst, What Evolution Is (New York, 2001: Perseus Book Group - Basic Books)

117. McDougall, Christopher, Born to Run: A Hidden Tribe, Superathletes, and the Greatest Race the World Has Never Seen (New York, 2009: Random House - Vintage)

118. McGrew, William C., "The Nature of Culture: Prospects and Pitfalls of Cultural Primatology" in de Waal, Frans B. M., editor, Tree of Origin: What Primate Behavior Can Tell Us about Human Social Evolution (Cambridge, Massachusetts, 2002: Harvard University Press)

119. Menino, Holly, Calls Beyond Our Hearing: Unlocking the Secrets of Animal Voices (New York, 2012: St. Martin's Press)

120. Merzenich, M. M. and de Charms, R. C., "Neural Representations, Experience, and Change" in Llinás, Rodolfo R. and Churchland, Patricia S., The Mind-Brain Continuum: Sensory Processes (Cambridge, Massachusetts, 1998: The MIT Press - Bradford Books)

121. Merriam - Webster Editorial Staff, Merriam - Webster's Eleventh Collegiate Dictionary, originally published in 1993 (Springfield, Massachusetts, 2004: Encyclopedia Britannica - Merriam-Webster)

122. Michel, Lou and Herbeck, Dan, American Terrorist: Timothy McVeigh and the Oklahoma City Bombing (New York, 2001: Harper-Collins - Regan Books)

123. Miles, H. Lyn, "Language and the Orang-utan", in Cavalieri, Paola and Singer, Peter, editors, The Great Ape Project: Equality Beyond Humanity (New York, 1993: St. Martin's - Griffin)

124. Moelling, Karin, Viruses: More Friends Than Foes (Singapore, 2017: World Scientific Publishing)

125. Moore, Cassandra and Cavanagh, Patrick, "Recovery of 3D volume from 2-tone images of novel objects", in Tarr, Michael J. and Bülthoff, Heinrich H., Object Recognition in Man, Monkey, and Machine (Boston, Massachusetts, 1998: The MIT Press)

126. Moore, Pete, $E = mc^2$: The Great Ideas that Shaped Our World (New York, 2002: Friedman/Fairfax)

127. Moose, Charles A., Three Weeks in October: The Manhunt for the Serial Sniper (New York, 2003: Penguin - Dutton)

128. Morris, Desmond, The Naked Ape (New York, 1999: Delta Books, Dell Publishing, Random House, Inc.)

129. Morris, Simon Conway, Life's Solution: Inevitable Humans in a Lonely Universe (New York, 2003: Cambridge University Press)

130. Morton, Alexandra, Listening to Whales: What the Orcas Have Taught Us (New York, 2002: Ballantine Books)

131. Noë, Alva, "Is the Visual World a Grand Illusion?", Journal of Consciousness Studies, No. 5-6 (Imprint Academic 2002)

132. Noback, Charles R., Strominger, Norman L., Demarest, Robert J., and Ruggiero, David A., The Human Nervous System: Structure and Function, Sixth Edition (Totowa, New Jersey, 2005: Humana Press)

133. "Oklahoma City," a PBS, American Experience Film, directed by Barak Goodman, first broadcast on February 7, 2017

134. Owens, Mark and Owens, Delia, Cry of the Kalahari (Boston, Massachusetts, 1984: Houghton Mifflin)

135. Pérez-Uribe, Andrés, "Of implementing neural epigenesis, reinforcement learning, and mental rehearsal in a mobile autonomous robot" (2000)

136. Park, "The Power of Sleep", Time, September 22, 2014, page 57.

137. Parker, Andrew, In the Blink of an Eye: How Vision Sparked the Big Bang of Evolution (New York, 2003: Perseus Books - Basic Books)

138. Peck, M. Scott, *People of the Lie: The Hope for Healing Human Evil* (New York, 1983: Simon and Schuster)

139. Physher, J. P., "FYI: Why are rainbows shaped like an arch?", *Popular Science*: April 2003

140. Pinker, Steven, *How the Mind Works* (New York, 1997: W. W. Norton)

141. Pryce-Jones, David, "The shame that haunts the Arab mind" (The Daily Telegraph, September 16, 2001, http://www.dailytelegraph.co.uk/ opinion/ main.jhtml?xml=/opinion/2001/09/16/do07.xml)

142. Pusey, Anne E., "Of Genes and Apes: Chimpanzee Social Organization and Reproduction", in de Waal, Frans B. M. and Tyack, Peter L., editors, *Animal Social Complexity: Intelligence, Culture, and Individualized Societies* (Cambridge, Massachusetts, 2003: Harvard University Press)

143. Ramachandran, V. S. and Blakeslee, Sandra, *Phantoms in the Brain: Probing the Mysteries of the Human Mind* (New York, 1998: HarperCollins - Quill)

144. Ramachandran, V. S. et al., "Illusions of Body Image: What They Reveal About Human Nature" in Llinás, Rodolfo R. and Churchland, Patricia S., *The Mind-Brain Continuum: Sensory Processes* (Cambridge, Massachusetts, 1998: The MIT Press - Bradford Books)

145. Ratey, John, *A User's Guide to the Brain: Perception, Attention, and the Four Theaters of the Brain* (New York, 2001: Vintage Books)

146. Redish, A. David, *The Mind Within the Brain: How We Make Decisions and How Those Decisions Go Wrong* (New York, 2013: Oxford University Press)

147. Restak, Richard, *Mysteries of the Mind* (Washington DC, 2000: National Geographic Society)

148. Rhodes, Richard, *Why They Kill: The Discoveries of a Maverick Criminologist* (New York, 1999: Alfred A. Knopf)

149. Robbins, Michael W., "Little People Make Big Splash", Discover, January 2005

150. Rollin, Bernard E., "The Ascent of Apes: Broadening the Moral Community", in Cavalieri, Paola and Singer, Peter, editors, The Great Ape Project: Equality Beyond Humanity (New York, 1993: St. Martin's - Griffin)

151. Sagan, Carl, The Dragons of Eden: Speculations on the Evolution of Human Intelligence (New York, 1977: Random House)

152. Samuel, Arthur, "Using Perceptual-Restoration Effects to Explore the Architecture of Perception" in Altmann, Gerry T. M., editor, Cognitive Models of Speech Processing: Psycholinguistic and Computational Perspectives (Cambridge, Massachusetts, 1995: The MIT Press - Bradford Books)

153. Scaggs, William, "New Neurons for New Memories", Scientific American Mind, September/October 2014, page 50.

154. Schusterman, Ronald J., Kastak, Colleen Reichmuth, and Kastak, David, "Equivalence Classification as an Approach to Social Knowledge: From Sea Lions to Simians" in de Waal, Frans B. M. and Tyack, Peter L., editors, Animal Social Complexity: Intelligence, Culture, and Individualized Societies (Cambridge, Massachusetts, 2003: Harvard University Press)

155. Seung, Sebastian, Connectome: How the Brain's Wiring Makes Us Who We Are (New York, 2012: Houghton Mifflin Harcourt)

156. Selfridge, Oliver G., "Pandemonium: A Paradigm for Learning" in Blake, D. V. and Uttley, A. M., Proceedings of the Symposium on Mechanisation of Thought Processes (London, 1959: Her Majesty's Stationery Office)

157. Shepherd, Gordon M., Neurobiology, Third Edition (New York, 1994: Oxford University Press)

158. Shubin, Neil, Your Inner Fish: A Journey into the 3.5-Billion-Year History of the Human Body (New York, 2008: Random House - Pantheon)

159. Stanford, Craig B., The Hunting Apes: Meat Eating and the Origins of Human Behavior (Princeton, New Jersey, 1999: Princeton University Press)

160. Stanford, Craig B., Upright: The Evolutionary Key to Becoming Human (New York, 2003: Houghton Mifflin Company)

161. Strum, Shirley C., Almost Human: A Journey into the World of Baboons (Chicago, Illinois, 2001: The University of Chicago Press)

162. Sun Tzu, The Art of War, Translated by Samuel B. Griffith, Collector's Edition (Norwalk, Connecticut, 1991: Easton Press)

163. Swisher, Carl C., Curtis, Garniss H., and Lewin, Roger, Java Man: How Two Geologists' Dramatic Discoveries Changed Our Understanding of the Evolutionary Path to Modern Humans (New York, 2000: Scribner)

164. Tattersall, Ian, The Fossil Trail: How we know what we think we know about human evolution (New York, 1995: Oxford University Press)

165. Tattersall, Ian, The Monkey in the Mirror: Essays on the Science of What Makes Us Human (New York, 2002: Harcourt Inc.)

166. Thatcher, Margaret, Statecraft: Strategies for a Changing World (New York, 2002: HarperCollins)

167. Thibodeau, David with Whiteson, Leon, A Place Called Waco: A Survivor's Story (New York, 1999: PublicAffairs, Perseus Book Group)

168. Thomas, Elizabeth Marshall, The Harmless People (New York, 1989: Random House - Vintage Books)

169. Thomas, Elizabeth Marshall, The Old Way: A Story of the First People (New York, 2006: Farrar, Straus and Giroux - Sarah Crichton Books)

170. Thomas, Lewis, The Lives of a Cell: Notes of a Biology Watcher (New York, 1986: New American Library)

171. Turnbull, Colin M., The Forest People (New York, 1962: Simon and Schuster - Touchstone Books)

172. Unwin, David M., The Pterosaurs from Deep Time (New York, 2006: Pearson Education, Inc. - Pi Press)

173. Van Der Post, Laurens, The Heart of the Hunter: Customs and Myths of the African Bushman (New York, 1989: Harcourt Brace & Company - Harvest Books)

174. Wade, Nicholas, Before the Dawn: Recovering the Lost History of our Ancestors (New York, 2006: Penguin Press)

175. Ward, Peter and Kirschvink, Joe, A New History of Life: The Radical New Discoveries about the Origins and Evolution of Life on Earth (New York, 2015: Bloomsbury Press)

176. Wells, Spencer, Pandora's Seed: The Unforeseen Cost of Civilization (New York, 2010: Random House)

177. Wells, Spencer, The Journey of Man: A Genetic Odyssey (Princeton, New Jersey, 2002: Princeton University Press)

178. Wilber, Ken, A Brief History of Everything (Boston, Massachusetts, 1996: Shambhala Publications, Inc.)

179. Wilkinson, Gerald S., "Social and Vocal Complexity in Bats" in de Waal, Frans B. M. and Tyack, Peter L., editors, Animal Social Complexity: Intelligence, Culture, and Individualized Societies (Cambridge, Massachusetts, 2003: Harvard University Press)

180. Wilkinson, Matt, Restless Creatures: The Story of Life in Ten Movements (New York, 2016: Perseus - Basic)

181. Wrangham, Richard and Peterson, Dale, Demonic Males: Apes and the Origins of Human Violence (New York, 1996: Houghton Mifflin - Mariner)

182. Zeman, Adam, Consciousness: A User's Guide (New Haven, Connecticut, 2002: Yale University Press)

Notes

1   Margulis, Symbiotic Planet, 30.

2   *The latest common ancestor of all extant living things lived 3.5 billion years ago.*
     Brown, The Energy of Life, 44.
     Dulbecco, The Design of Life, 425.
     Margulis and Sagan, Microcosms, 11, 107.
     Dawkins, The Ancestor's Tale, 7.
     Margulis and Sagan, What is Life? 58, 88-89.

3   *The fundamental property of life is the transformation of sensation into movement.*
     Llinás, i of the vortex, 13, 14, 26, 38, 51, 78.
     Zeman, Consciousness, 67, 187, 295.
     de Waal, The Ape and the Sushi Master, 219.
     Churchland, Neurophilosophy, 1, 62.
     Gellatly and Zarate, Introducing Mind and Brain, 57.
     Seung, Connectome, 52.
     Goodale and Humphrey, "The Objects of Action and Perception" in Tarr and Bülthoff, Object Recognition in Man, Monkey, and Machine, 182.
     Shepherd, Neurobiology, 103, 381, 516.
     Dehaene, Consciousness and the Brain, 51, 188-189.
     Mayer, The Mind-Gut Connection, 160.
     Margulis and Sagan, What is Life? 166, 224.
     Dulbecco, The Design of Life, 340, 364.

4   *Violence, sex, and work are fundamental issues of all forms of life.*
     Ardrey, The Territorial Imperative.
     Morris, The Naked Ape, 35, 39.
     Lorenz, On Aggression, 43, 67, 89, 98-99, 104-105, 109.

LeDoux, Synaptic Self, 8-9, 206-207, 303, 321.

Damasio, Descartes' Error, 109-110, 114-115, 225.

Damasio, Looking for Spinoza, 50.

Damasio, Self Comes to Mind, 114.

Llinás, i of the vortex, 145, 225.

Ramachandran and Blakeslee, Phantoms in the Brain, 177-178.

Churchland, Neurophilosophy, 1, 88-89.

Churchland, A Neurocomputational Perspective, 207.

Churchland, The Engine of Reason, the Seat of the Soul, 5.

Sagan, The Dragons of Eden, 29.

Dulbecco, The Design of Life, 150, 315, 319, 326, 328-329, 339, 434.

Johanson and Edey, Lucy, 326.

Peck, People of the Lie.

Aristotle, Politics.

Diamond, Guns, Germs, and Steel.

Diamond, The World Until Yesterday, 335.

Faludi, Stiffed, 423-424.

Parker, In the Blink of an Eye, 231.

Ratey, A User's Guide to the Brain, 65, 228.

Fouts and Mills, Next of Kin, 81.

Grandin and Johnson, Animals in Translation, 47, 204.

Keen, Fire in the Belly, 7, 27, 34, 52, 70.

Kurzweil, How to Create a Mind, 105.

Ghiglieri, The Dark Side of Man, 13.

de Waal and Tyack, Animal Social Complexity, 90.

Morris, Life's Solution, 183-185.

Griffin, The Question of Animal Awareness, 3.

Dawkins, The Ancestor's Tale, 466.

Shepherd, Neurobiology, 478, 544-545, 562.

Noback, Strominger, Demarest, and Ruggiero, The Human Nervous System, 373-374.

Margulis, Symbiotic Planet, 9.

Margulis and Sagan, Microcosms, 17.

Margulis and Sagan, What is Life? 1, 30, 123.

Menino, Calls Beyond Our Hearing, 19, 35, 93.

Morton, Listening to Whales, 122-123.

Thomas, The Lives of a Cell, 99.

Bejan and Zane, Design in Nature, 257.

Unwin, The Pterosaurs from Deep Time, 167.

Ward and Kirschvink, A New History of Life, 113.

Brown, The Energy of Life, 137, 138.

Kilmartin, The Masculine Self, viii.

Park, "The Power of Sleep", Time, September 22, 2014, page 57.

Dixson, "Lost at Sea", Scientific American, June 2017, 43.

Carter, Mapping the Mind, 98.

Harari, Sapiens, 25.

Wilkinson, Restless Creatures, 4.

Mayer, The Mind-Gut Connection, 44.

Brodal, The Central Nervous System, 397, 405.

Horwitz, War of the Whales, 175, 302.

5   Moelling, Viruses, 23.

Dulbecco, The Design of Life, 17.

Griggs, "Dead or Alive: What's the Meaning of Life?", Popular Science, Summer 2018, 10.

6   See note 3.

7   *The brain contains a world model.*

Lorenz, The Natural Science of the Human Species, xxvi-xxvii, xxx, 13, 17-22.

de Waal, The Ape and the Sushi Master, 96.

Llinás, i of the vortex, 3, 13, 14, 24, 38, 39-40, 41, 55, 65, 81-82, 108-109, 135, 181, 259.

LeDoux, Synaptic Self, 176.

Goodale and Humphrey, "The Objects of Action and Perception" in Tarr and Bülthoff, Object Recognition in Man, Monkey, and Machine, 181-182, 195.

Moore and Cavanagh, "Recovery of 3D volume from 2-tone images of novel objects" in Tarr and Bülthoff, Object Recognition in Man, Monkey, and Machine, 60.

Davenport, From Mind to Brain Machine.

Keijzer, Representation and Behavior, 40, 68.

Perez-Uribe, "Of implementing neural epigenesis".

Albus, The Engineering of Mind.

Shepherd, Neurobiology, 381, 490.

Damasio, Descartes' Error, 240.

Damasio, The Feeling of What Happens, 322.

Damasio, Self Comes to Mind, 64.

Dulbecco, The Design of Life, 338.

Morris, Life's Solution, 178.

Churchland, Neurophilosophy, 1-2.

Llinás and Pare, "The Brain as a Closed System Modulated by the Senses" in Llinás and Churchland, The Mind-Brain Continuum, 2, 3, 5.

Ramachandran and Blakeslee, Phantoms in the Brain, 59.

Gazzaniga, Ivry, and Mangun, Cognitive Neuroscience, 401.

Hawkins and Blakeslee, On Intelligence, 6.

Pinker, How the Mind Works, 333.

Harnish, Minds, Brains, Computers, 49.

Kortlandt, "Spirits Dressed in Furs?" in Cavalieri and Singer, The Great Ape Project, 138-140.

Hofstadter and Sander, Surfaces and Essences, 68.

Griffin, The Question of Animal Awareness, 13-14.

Menino, Calls Beyond Our Hearing, 45.

Rhodes, Why They Kill, 56-57.

Redish, The Mind Within the Brain, 10.

Drea and Frank, "The Social Complexity of Spotted Hyenas" in de Waal and Tyack, Animal Social Complexity, 146.

Berman, "Body of Work", Discover, July/August 2014.

Macknik and Martinez-Conde, "What a Trip", Scientific American Mind, May/June 2014, 66-67.

Scaggs, "New Neurons for New Memories", Scientific American Mind, September/October 2014, 50.

Dehaene, Reading in the Brain, 268.

Thomas, The Lives of a Cell, 90.

8   See note 4.

9   Damasio, Self Comes to Mind, 64.

10   Damasio, Descartes' Error, 239.

11   Lorenz, The Natural Science of the Human Species, 172-173.

Zeman, Consciousness, 294.

Merzenich and de Charms, "Neural Representations, Experience, and Change" in Llinás and Churchland, The Mind-Brain Continuum, 62.
Dehaene, Reading in the Brain, 130-132.

12   Damasio, Descartes' Error, 102-103, 105.

13   Churchland, The Engine of Reason, the Seat of the Soul, 100.

14   Damasio, Looking for Spinoza, 107.
Damasio, Descartes' Error, 87.

15   Brown, The Energy of Life, 143-145.

16   See note 3.

17   See note 4.

18   See note 3.

19   Brown, The Energy of Life, 8.

20   Hofstadter, Godel, Escher, Bach, 528-529.

21   See note 3.

22   Dulbecco, The Design of Life, 87, 97.

23   Brown, The Energy of Life, 16.

24   Lane, The Vital Question, 89.

25   Hofstadter, Godel, Escher, Bach, 529.
Shepherd, Neurobiology, 47.

26   Brown, The Energy of Life, xi, 17-18, 24, 36-37.
Hoffman, Life's Ratchet, 121-122, 138.

27   Morris, Life's Solution, 38.
Thomas, The Lives of a Cell, 143-144.
Margulis and Sagan, Microcosms, 55, 137.
Margulis, Symbiotic Planet, 71.
Margulis and Sagan, What is Life? 85.
Brown, The Energy of Life, 15.

28   Brown, The Energy of Life, 8.

29   Lane, The Vital Question, 63.

30   Brown, The Energy of Life, 16.

31   Brown, The Energy of Life, 8.

32   Brown, The Energy of Life, 38.

33   Brown, The Energy of Life, 24.

34   Brown, The Energy of Life, 16.

35   Brown, The Energy of Life, 4, 15.

36   Zeman, Consciousness, 56.

37   Ramachandran and Blakeslee, Phantoms in the Brain, 152.

LeDoux, Synaptic Self, 28.

Damasio, The Feeling of What Happens, 300.

Grandin and Johnson, Animals in Translation, 66.

Koch, The Quest for Consciousness, 206, 235-236.

38   Damasio, Descartes' Error, 29.

LeDoux, Synaptic Self, 40.

Llinás, i of the vortex, 120.

Restak, Mysteries of the Mind, 5, 11-12.

39   *The cranial brain comprises four layers.*

Churchland, Neurophilosophy, 62.

MacLean, The Triune Brain in Evolution.

Grandin and Johnson, Animals in Translation, 54.

Sagan, The Dragons of Eden, 55-57.

Damasio, Descartes' Error, 191.

Damasio, The Feeling of What Happens, 55 (table.), 174 (table.), 199 (table.).

Damasio, Self Comes to Mind, 181-182.

Wilber, A Brief History of Everything.

Grossman, On Killing, 37.

Maslow, Motivation and Personality.

Boeree, "Abraham Maslow", 2.

Berne, Games People Play.

Eccles, Evolution of the Brain, 71-72, 73 (fig.), 184 (fig.), 204 (fig.), 232 (fig.).

Dawkins, The Selfish Gene, 11.

Mayr, What Evolution Is, 131.

Darwin, The Origin of Species, 227.

Ratey, A User's Guide to the Brain, 115, 172, 337-346.

Shepherd, Neurobiology, 392.

Ghiglieri, The Dark Side of Man, 35.

Freud, Beyond the Pleasure Principle.

Redish, The Mind Within the Brain, 44.

Selfridge, "Pandemonium: A Paradigm for Learning" in Blake and Uttley, Proceedings of the Symposium on Mechanisation of Thought Processes, 511-531.

40   Damasio, The Feeling of What Happens, 36, 291.
      Damasio, Looking for Spinoza, 28, 49, 148.

41   Damasio, Descartes' Error, 109-110.

42   Llinás, i of the vortex, 15.
      Churchland, Neurophilosophy, 13.
      Brodal, The Central Nervous System, 104, 121.

43   See note 3.

44   See note 7.

45   Damasio, Self Comes to Mind, 64.

46   Carter, Mapping the Mind, 204.
      Llinás, i of the vortex, 6.

47   Pinker, How the Mind Works, 191, 213.
      Lorenz, The Natural Science of the Human Species, 59-60.

48   Malsburg, "The Binding Problem of Neural Networks" in Llinás and
      Churchland, The Mind-Brain Continuum, 143.
      Wells, Pandora's Seed, 85.

49   Damasio, Descartes' Error, 104.
      Churchland, A Neurocomputational Perspective, 191.
      Grandin and Johnson, Animals in Translation, 102.

50   Zeman, Consciousness, 56.

51   Grandin and Johnson, Animals in Translation, 263.
      Dehaene, Reading in the Brain, 42.

52   Damasio, Descartes' Error, 97.
      Pinker, How the Mind Works, 270-271, 333.
      Llinás, i of the vortex, 135.
      Noë, "Is the Visual World a Grand Illusion?", Journal of
      Consciousness Studies, No. 5-6.
      Lorenz, The Natural Science of the Human Species, 36.
      Ramachandran, "Illusions of Body Image" in Llinás and Churchland,
      The Mind-Brain Continuum, 42.

53   See note 3.

54   *Evolution is blind, incremental, and accretive.*
      Fouts and Mills, Next of Kin, 55, 57, 105.
      Gould and McKay, Encyclopedia of Mammals, 39.
      Tattersall, The Monkey in the Mirror, 72, 126-127.
      Robbins, "Little People Make Big Splash", Discover, January 2005, 31.

Lorenz, On Aggression, 228.

Johanson and Edey, Lucy, 100.

Goodall, In the Shadow of Man, 37.

Dawkins, The Ancestor's Tale, 103.

McGrew, "The Nature of Culture" in de Waal, Tree of Origin, 240.

de Duve, Life Evolving, 191.

Grandin and Johnson, Animals in Translation, 244-245.

Atkins and Beran, General Chemistry, 126.

Sagan, The Dragons of Eden, 57.

55   See note 39.

56   Damasio, Descartes' Error, 109-110.

57   Damasio, Self Comes to Mind, 64.

58   Rhodes, Why They Kill, 54, 82.

Churchland, Neurophilosophy, 1.

Davenport, From Mind to Brain Machine.

59   *The brain makes avatars that represent the family.*

Rhodes, Why They Kill, 54.

de Waal, The Ape and the Sushi Master, 29.

Pinker, How the Mind Works, 192.

Fouts and Mills, Next of Kin, 236.

Churchland, Neurophilosophy, 1.

Davenport, From Mind to Brain Machine.

60   Grandin and Johnson, Animals in Translation, 28-30, 72-73.

Wrangham and Peterson, Demonic Males, 256.

Pinker, How the Mind Works, 353.

Moose, Three Weeks in October, 298.

Boesch, "Complex Cooperation among Taï Chimpanzees" in de Waal and Tyack, Animal Social Complexity, 108.

Goodall, In the Shadow of Man, 141.

Blum, Love at Goon Park, 183.

61   Damasio, Descartes' Error, xii-xiii, 222.

62   Ramachandran and Blakeslee, Phantoms in the Brain, 67, 134.

Ramachandran, "Illusions of Body Image" in Llinás and Churchland, The Mind-Brain Continuum, 41.

Shepherd, Neurobiology, 376-378.

Damasio and Damasio, "Making Images and Creating Subjectivity" in Llinás and Churchland, The Mind-Brain Continuum, 20.

Damasio, The Feeling of What Happens, 80, 321-322.

Damasio, Descartes' Error, 100.

Brodal, The Central Nervous System, 46, 138.

Carter, Mapping the Mind, 132, 168.

63   Parker, In the Blink of an Eye, 93, 221, 232-233, 272, 287-289.

64   Grandin and Johnson, 263.

Dehaene, Reading in the Brain, 42.

65   Livingstone, Vision and Art, 192-194.

Gould and McKay, Encyclopedia of Mammals, 132.

Grandin and Johnson, Animals in Translation, 19, 41, 44, 61.

Pinker, How the Mind Works, 183, 287.

Llinás, i of the vortex, 104.

Ramachandran and Blakeslee, Phantoms in the Brain, 71-72.

Glynn, An Anatomy of Thought, 148-149.

Brodal, The Central Nervous System, 186.

66   *The brain discards a lot of data.*

Ramachandran and Blakeslee, Phantoms in the Brain, 66.

Pinker, How the Mind Works, 84.

Moore, $E = mc^2$, 16.

Brown, Bury My Heart at Wounded Knee, 289.

Zeman, Consciousness, 186.

Johanson and Edey, Lucy, 164.

Shepherd, Neurobiology, 65.

Glynn, An Anatomy of Thought, 159.

Carter, Mapping the Mind, 146.

Lorenz, The Natural Science of the Human Species, 57, 58, 173.

Llinás, i of the vortex, 24, 108, 220.

Grandin and Johnson, Animals in Translation, 65, 67, 218.

Churchland, A Neurocomputational Perspective, 266.

67   *The brain interpolates, sees what it expects to see, and confabulates.*

Redish, The Mind Within the Brain, 5.

Ramachandran and Blakeslee, Phantoms in the Brain, 89, 103, 104, 106.

Samuel, "Using Perceptual-Restoration Effects to Explore the Architecture of Perception" in Altmann, Cognitive Models of Speech Processing, 295.

Grandin and Johnson, Animals in Translation, 51, 100,266, 303.

Dehaene, Reading in the Brain, 49.

Fields, The Other Brain, 235.

Conway, Cognitive Models of Memory, 261.

Carter, Mapping the Mind, 106, 168.

68 Lorenz, The Natural Science of the Human Species, 31, 58-59, 63, 64.

Gazzaniga, Ivry, and Mangun, Cognitive Neuroscience, 340.

Katz, The Biggest Bangs, 83.

Johanson and Edey, Lucy, 257.

69 Zeman, Consciousness, 68.

70 Ramachandran and Blakeslee, Phantoms in the Brain, 72, 77.

Zeman, Consciousness, 155, 226.

Gazzaniga, Ivry, and Mangun, Cognitive Neuroscience, 62, 160.

Churchland, Neurophilosophy, 121.

Noback, Strominger, Demarest, and Ruggiero, The Human Nervous System, 448.

71 Lorenz, The Natural Science of the Human Species, 172-173.

Zeman, Consciousness, 294.

Llinás and Churchland, The Mind-Brain Continuum, 62.

Dehaene, Reading in the Brain, 130.

72 Churchland, The Engine of Reason, the Seat of the Soul, 100.

73 Damasio, Descartes' Error, 102-103, 105.

74 Damasio and Damasio, "Making Images and Creating Subjectivity" in Llinás and Churchland, The Mind-Brain Continuum, 20.

Damasio, Descartes' Error, 98, 101.

75 Carter, Mapping the Mind, 174.

76 Shepherd, Neurobiology, 65.

Glynn, An Anatomy of Thought, 159.

Zeman, Consciousness, 215.

Ramachandran and Blakeslee, Phantoms in the Brain, 77.

Damasio, The Feeling of What Happens, 220.

77 See note 4.

78 LeDoux, Synaptic Self, 194, 206.

Damasio, Looking for Spinoza, 54.

Grandin and Johnson, Animals in Translation, 198.

Kramer, Beyond Max Weber, 5.

Damasio, Descartes' Error, 53.

Llinás, i of the vortex, 57.

Wrangham and Peterson, Demonic Males, 188.

79   Dunbar and Barrett, Cousins, 205.

80   Kruuk, Niko's Nature, 188.

81   Lorenz, On Aggression, 116-117.

82   Damasio, The Feeling of What Happens, 106.

83   Shepherd, Neurobiology, 193.

84   Damasio, Descartes' Error, 88.

85   Johnson, "The Brain and Emotions", Discover, March 2003, 36.

Grandin and Johnson, Animals in Translation, 204, 213, 215-216.

Carter, Mapping the Mind, 97.

Damasio, Descartes' Error, 139.

86   Grandin and Johnson, Animals in Translation, 105-106, 108-109, 155.

Grossman, On Killing, xxviii, 29.

Lorenz, On Aggression, 31, 216.

87   Rhodes, Why They Kill, 53, 56.

Cavalieri and Singer, The Great Ape Project, 140.

Damasio, Self Comes to Mind, 64.

88   LeDoux, Synaptic Self, 27.

Churchland, The Engine of Reason, the Seat of the Soul, 268.

Damasio and Damasio, "Making Images and Creating Subjectivity" in Llinás and Churchland, The Mind-Brain Continuum, 22.

Lorenz, On Aggression, 167.

89   See note 2.

90   Physher, "FYI: Why are rainbows shaped like an arch?", Popular Science, April 2003, 100.

91   Grandin and Johnson, Animals in Translation, 260.

Goodall, In the Shadow of Man, 54.

Thomas, The Old Way, 172-173.

92   Llinás, i of the vortex, 23.

Damasio, The Feeling of What Happens, 305, 308.

Hofstadter, Godel, Escher, Bach, 388.

Brodal, The Central Nervous System, 346.

93   Damasio, Self Comes to Mind, 64.

94   See note 39.

95   Damasio, The Feeling of What Happens, Chapters 5, 6, and 7.

96   Damasio, The Feeling of What Happens, 106, 267.
      Damasio, Self Comes to Mind, 224, 311.

97   Damasio, The Feeling of What Happens, 154, 156, 155-159, 180-181,
      236-240, 248-250, 260-261.

98   Damasio, Descartes' Error, 88.

99   Damasio, The Feeling of What Happens, 221, 228.

100   Damasio, The Feeling of What Happens, 180-181.

101   de Waal and Aureli, "Conflict Resolution and Distress Alleviation
      in Monkeys and Apes" in Carter, Lederhendler, and Kilpatrick, The
      Integrative Neurobiology of Affiliation, 119-120, 123-124.
      Lopez, Of Wolves and Men, 89, 104-105.
      Pinker, How the Mind Works, 505.

102   *The brain makes a lot of assumptions.*
      Ramachandran and Blakeslee, Phantoms in the Brain, 68.
      Pinker, How the Mind Works, 28-30, 213.
      LeDoux, Synaptic Self, 203.
      Mallot and Allen, Computational Vision, 14.
      Dawkins, The Ancestor's Tale, 393.
      Carter, Mapping the Mind, 131.
      Churchland, Neurophilosophy, 264.
      Atkins and Beran, General Chemistry, 275.
      Gärdenfors, Conceptual Spaces, 203.
      Hofstadter, Godel, Escher, Bach, 386.
      Brodal, The Central Nervous System, 190-191.
      Grandin and Johnson, Animals in Translation, 98.

103   Damasio, The Feeling of What Happens, 16.

104   Goodall, In the Shadow of Man, 242, 247-248.

105   *Ethics, altruism, and the conscience are results of internal dialogs with the
      family.*
      Rhodes, Why They Kill, 54, 82.
      Churchland, Neurophilosophy, 1.
      Davenport, From Mind to Brain Machine.

106   Damasio, The Feeling of What Happens, 189.

Restak, Mysteries of the Mind, 145.

Fouts and Fouts, "Chimpanzees' Use of Sign Language" in Cavalieri and Singer, The Great Ape Project, 34.

Gellatly and Zarate, Introducing Mind and Brain, 77.

Rhodes, Why They Kill, 82, 84, 274.

Koch, The Quest for Consciousness, 75.

107   Margulis and Sagan, Microcosms, 150-151.

108   Damasio, Self Comes to Mind, 257.

109   Zeman, Consciousness, 56.

110   Thomas, The Lives of a Cell, 140-141.

111   Dunbar and Barrett, Cousins, 211.

Strum, Almost Human, 167.

Pinker, How the Mind Works, 305.

Clark, "Apes and the Idea of Kindred" in Cavalieri and Singer, The Great Ape Project, 123-124.

Churchland, Neurophilosophy, 315.

Llinás and Pare, "The Brain as a Closed System Modulated by the Senses" in Llinás and Churchland, The Mind-Brain Continuum, 5.

112   Rhodes, Why They Kill, 58.

113   *A large part of the brain is devoted to vision.*

Ramachandran and Blakeslee, Phantoms in the Brain, 72, 77.

Zeman, Consciousness, 155, 226.

Gazzaniga, Ivry, and Mangun, Cognitive Neuroscience, 62, 160.

Churchland, Neurophilosophy, 121.

Noback, Strominger, Demarest, and Ruggiero, The Human Nervous System, 448.

114   *The brain can store tens of thousands of objects.*

Grandin and Johnson, Animals in Translation, 263.

Dehaene, Reading in the Brain, 42.

115   Damasio, Self Comes to Mind, 64.

116   Damasio, Descartes' Error, 88.

117   *The state of the body is conveyed to the brain via the nervous system and the bloodstream.*

Damasio, Looking for Spinoza, 107.

Damasio, Descartes' Error, 87.

118   *The brain uses networks of neurons to store information.*
        Lorenz, The Natural Science of the Human Species, 172-173.
        Zeman, Consciousness, 294.
        Merzenich and de Charms, "Neural Representations, Experience, and Change" in Llinás and Churchland, The Mind-Brain Continuum, 62.
        Dehaene, Reading in the Brain, 130-132.

119   Damasio and Damasio, "Making Images and Creating Subjectivity" in Llinás and Churchland, The Mind-Brain Continuum, 23.

120   Damasio, Descartes' Error, 100, 226-227, 239, 240.
        Damasio, The Feeling of What Happens, 191, 224.
        LeDoux, Synaptic Self, 256.

121   Damasio, The Feeling of What Happens, 12.

122   Damasio, Descartes' Error, 239.
        Damasio, The Feeling of What Happens, 228.
        de Waal, The Ape and the Sushi Master, 309.

123   Carter, Mapping the Mind, 168.
        Stanford, Upright, 105-106.
        Graham and Beard, Eyelids of Morning, 198.
        Redish, The Mind Within the Brain, 112, 155.

124   Damasio, Descartes' Error, 102-103, 105.

125   Wrangham and Peterson, Demonic Males, 179-180.
        Llinás, i of the vortex, 51.

126   Damasio, Self Comes to Mind, 257.

127   Zeman, Consciousness, 56.

128   Wrangham and Peterson, Demonic Males, 179-180.
        Llinás, i of the vortex, 51.

129   See note 3.

130   Carter, Mapping the Mind, 168.
        Stanford, Upright, 105-106.
        Graham and Beard, Eyelids of Morning, 198.
        Redish, The Mind Within the Brain, 112, 155.

131   Ramachandran and Blakeslee, Phantoms in the Brain, 151, 155, 156.

132   Noback, Strominger, Demarest, and Ruggiero, The Human Nervous System, 20, 53.
        LeDoux, Synaptic Self, 47.

133   Shepherd, Neurobiology, 102.

134 Llinás, i of the vortex, 229-231.

  Lorenz, On Aggression, 175.

135 Carter, Mapping the Mind, 23.

  Fouts and Mills, Next of Kin, 91.

136 *All living things possess a sense of self.*

  LeDoux, Synaptic Self, 27.

  Churchland, The Engine of Reason, the Seat of the Soul, 268.

  Damasio and Damasio, "Making Images and Creating Subjectivity" in Llinás and Churchland, The Mind-Brain Continuum, 22.

  Lorenz, On Aggression, 167.

137 Damasio, Self Comes to Mind, 172.

138 Hofstadter, Godel, Escher, Bach, 386.

139 Grandin and Johnson, Animals in Translation, 272-273.

  Ghiglieri, The Dark Side of Man, 171.

  Swisher, Curtis and Lewin, Java Man, 176.

  Goodall, Through a Window, 14.

  Schusterman, Kastak, and Kastak, "Equivalence Classification as an Approach to Social Knowledge: From Sea Lions to Simians" in de Waal and Tyack, Animal Social Complexity, 179.

  Miles, "Language and the Orang-utan," in Cavalieri and Singer, The Great Ape Project, 49.

  Fouts and Mills, Next of Kin, 73, 82, 157, 293.

140 Fouts and Mills, Next of Kin, 194-195.

141 Fouts and Mills, Next of Kin, 102, 242, 349, 377.

  Rollin, "The Ascent of Apes: Broadening the Moral Community," in Cavalieri and Singer, The Great Ape Project, 214.

142 Darwin, The Origin of Species, 227.

  Damasio, Descartes' Error, 260.

  Wade, Before the Dawn, 7, 19.

143 Lorenz, On Aggression, 165-166.

144 Goodall, In the Shadow of Man, 245.

  Grandin and Johnson, Animals in Translation, 130.

  Lorenz, On Aggression, 216.

145 Dunbar, "Brains on Two Legs," in de Waal and Tyack, Animal Social Complexity, 182.

  Stanford, The Hunting Apes, 177.

Wilkinson, "Social and Vocal Complexity in Bats" in de Waal and Tyack, Animal Social Complexity, 324.

Goodall, In the Shadow of Man, 120.

146   Lorenz, On Aggression, 165-166.

147   de Waal, The Ape and the Sushi Master, 47, 300.

Goodall, In the Shadow of Man, 71, 124.

Grandin and Johnson, Animals in Translation, 164.

Stanford, The Hunting Apes, 88.

148   Comer, Internetworking With TCP/IP, 105, 106-107.

Hofstadter, Godel, Escher, Bach, 170, 171, 300.

149   See note 39.

150   See note 105.

151   *The original humans lived 50,000 years ago.*

Dunbar and Barrett, Cousins, 216.

Diamond, Guns, Germs, and Steel, 39.

de Duve, Life Evolving, 193.

Wells, Pandora's Seed, 14, 15-16, 37, 39-40, 80, 101-102.

Wells, The Journey of Man, 54, 60, 92-93, 107, 149.

Thomas, The Old Way, 65.

Wade, Before the Dawn, 1, 7-9, 29, 107.

Morris, Life's Solution, 274.

McDougall, Born to Run, 229.

Tattersall, The Fossil Trail, 218, 225, 245.

Baggott, Origins, 354.

Margulis and Sagan, Microcosms, 231, 233.

Dawkins, The Ancestor's Tale, 35.

152   Thomas, The Harmless People, 6.

153   Thomas, The Harmless People, 6.

Van Der Post, The Heart of the Hunter, 6.

Turnbull, The Forest People, 35.

154   Thomas, The Harmless People, 6.

155   Van Der Post, The Heart of the Hunter, 60.

156   *The optimal number of members in an extended family of humans is 150.*

Fouts and Mills, Next of Kin, 61-62.

Pusey, "Of Genes and Apes: Chimpanzee Social Organization and Reproduction," in de Waal and Tyack, Animal Social Complexity, 34.

Diamond, Guns, Germs, and Steel, 271.

Dunbar, "Brains on Two Legs: Group Size and the Evolution of Intelligence" in de Waal, Tree of Origin: What Primate Behavior Can Tell Us about Human Social Evolution, 180-181.

Tattersall, The Monkey in the Mirror, 199.

Ghiglieri, The Dark Side of Man, 69.

Wrangham and Peterson, Demonic Males, 65.

Thibodeau and Whiteson, A Place Called Waco, 189.

Goodman, "Oklahoma City" a PBS, American Experience Film.

Wells, Pandora's Seed, 38-39, 118-119, 205.

Wade, Before the Dawn, 16, 44, 58-60, 142, 160.

Tattersall, The Fossil Trail, 145.

Harari, Sapiens, 26-27.

157   Thomas, The Old Way, 139.

Tattersall, The Fossil Trail, 200.

158   Thomas, The Old Way, 167-168.

Thomas, The Harmless People, 198.

159   *The original humans ate a wide variety of foods.*

Wells, Pandora's Seed, 84-85.

Mayer, The Mind-Gut Connection, 201.

Thomas, The Old Way, 106, 110.

Wade, Before the Dawn, 67.

160   Thomas, The Harmless People, 172-173.

161   Wells, The Journey of Man, 158.

162   Wells, The Journey of Man, 158-159.

163   Ghiglieri, The Dark Side of Man, 141.

Wells, The Journey of Man, 159.

Stanford, The Hunting Apes, 158-159.

Thomas, The Old Way, 228.

164   Wells, The Journey of Man, 159.

165   Thomas, The Old Way, 195-196.

Wade, Before the Dawn, 68.

166   Thomas, The Old Way, 107, 119, 121.

167   Gould and McKay, Encyclopedia of Mammals, 201-202.

Pinker, How the Mind Works, 375.

168   Thomas, The Old Way, 98.

169   *Humans are designed to walk and run great distances.*
   Sagan, The Dragons of Eden, 191-192.
   Thomas, The Old Way, 29-33.
   Thomas, The Harmless People, 7.
   Turnbull, The Forest People, 14.
   McDougall, Born to Run, 15, 220-223, 225-229, 232, 235-236, 239.
   Wilkinson, Restless Creatures, 33, 34.

170   Calaprice, The Expanded Quotable Einstein, 202, 203.
   Cropper, Great Physicists, 18, 36, 150-151, 174-175.
   Greene, The Elegant Universe, 117.
   Damasio, Looking for Spinoza, 273.

171   Damasio, Looking for Spinoza, 160.
   Damasio, Descartes' Error, 261.
   Lorenz, The Natural Science of the Human Species, 79.
   Lorenz, On Aggression, 165.
   Peck, People of the Lie, 224-225.
   Hofstadter, Godel, Escher, Bach, 303.

172   Brown, The Energy of Life, 8.

173   Keen, Fire in the Belly, 32.
   Turnbull, The Forest People, 14.

174   See note 151.

175   See note 169.

176   See note 156.

177   Stanford, The Hunting Apes, 59.
   Wrangham and Peterson, Demonic Males, 166-167.
   Wade, Before the Dawn, 65.

178   Stanford, The Hunting Apes, 182.

179   Faludi, Stiffed, 143-144.
   Pinker, How the Mind Works, 364.
   Pryce-Jones, "The shame that haunts the Arab mind", The Daily Telegraph, September 16, 2001.

180   Peck, People of the Lie, 42, 120, 121, 125, 126, 218, 240, 249, 250, 253.
   Bly, The Sibling Society, 16-17.
   Thatcher, Statecraft, 288.
   Redish, The Mind Within the Brain, 208.

181   Goodall, Through a Window, 77-80.

182   Hare, Without Conscience, xi, 34.

183   Hare, Without Conscience, 74, 87.

184   Hare, Without Conscience, 87.

185   Hare, Without Conscience, 136, 142, 170, 175, 199.
       Damasio, Descartes' Error, 177-178.

186   Hare, Without Conscience, xi.
       Damasio, Descartes' Error, 177-178.
       Redish, The Mind Within the Brain, 130.

187   Hare, Without Conscience, 97.

188   Hare, Without Conscience, 136, 142, 215.
       Damasio, Descartes' Error, 177-178.

189   Hare, Without Conscience, 136, 142, 170, 175, 199.

190   Bly, Iron John, 180-181.
       Keen, Fire in the Belly, 29-31.
       Lorenz, On Aggression, 193.
       Kilmartin, The Masculine Self, 162.
       Wrangham and Peterson, Demonic Males, 190.
       Turnbull, The Forest People, 21.

191   Rhodes, Why They Kill, 81-82, 112.

192   Grossman, On Killing, 21-22, 25, 160.
       Rhodes, Why They Kill, 291– 294.

193   Grossman, On Killing, 35, 181.
       Rhodes, Why They Kill, 291– 294.
       Peck, People of the Lie, 240.

194   Bly, Iron John, 95.
       Ghiglieri, The Dark Side of Man, 139.

195   Rhodes, Why They Kill, 119.

196   Rhodes, Why They Kill, 119, 136.

197   Ishida, The Remains of War, 97, 93.

198   Rhodes, Why They Kill, 64, 112.

199   Rhodes, Why They Kill, 112-113, 120.

200   Rhodes, Why They Kill, 118.

201   Rhodes, Why They Kill, 120.

202   Rhodes, Why They Kill, 121.

203   Rhodes, Why They Kill, 121.

204   Rhodes, Why They Kill, 123.

205   Rhodes, Why They Kill, 122.

206   Rhodes, Why They Kill, 123.

207   Bly, Iron John, 95.

       Ghiglieri, The Dark Side of Man, 139.

208   *Television violence causes violent behavior in its viewers.*

       Grossman, On Killing, xix, 328-329.

       Bly, The Sibling Society, 139-140, 185-186.

       Damasio, The Feeling of What Happens, 188.

       Moose, Three Weeks in October, 225.

       Pinker, How the Mind Works, 29.

       Carter, Mapping the Mind, 125.

       Ghiglieri, The Dark Side of Man, 127.

       Kilmartin, The Masculine Self, 241-242.

209   TV History Website, "Annual_TV_Households_50-78.JPG".

210   Grossman, On Killing, 35, 181.

       Rhodes, Why They Kill, 291 – 294.

211   See note 208.

212   Bly, Iron John, 154, 197.

       Grossman, On Killing, 227, 272-273, 277, 284.

213   Rhodes, Why They Kill, 81-82, 112.

214   See note 156.

215   Keen, Fire in the Belly, 137.

       Blum, Love at Goon Park, 221, 279, 287.

       Dawkins, The Selfish Gene, 117.

       Stanford, The Hunting Apes, 182.

216   Grossman, On Killing, 175.

217   Ghiglieri, The Dark Side of Man, 11, 15.

       Wrangham and Peterson, Demonic Males, 109, 111, 119-120, 180-181.

218   Michel and Herbeck, American Terrorist, 163-164, 217.

219   See note 4.

220   See note 2.

221   Damasio, Looking for Spinoza, 37-38, 49

       Damasio, Self Comes to Mind, 26.

       Noback, Strominger, Demarest, and Ruggiero, The Human Nervous System, 121.

       Shubin, Your Inner Fish, 7.

Dehaene, Consciousness and the Brain, 162-163.

222   See note 4.

223   See note 156.

224   See note 169.

225   Wells, Pandora's Seed, 84-85.

       Mayer, The Mind-Gut Connection, 201.

226   Thomas, The Old Way, 106, 110.

       Wade, Before the Dawn, 67.

227   Thomas, The Old Way, 135, 232.

       Van Der Post, The Heart of the Hunter, 116.